CAMBRIDGE LIBRARY COLLECTION

Books of enduring scholarly value

Perspectives from the Royal Asiatic Society

A long-standing European fascination with Asia, from the Middle East to China and Japan, came more sharply into focus during the early modern period, as voyages of exploration gave rise to commercial enterprises such as the East India companies, and their attendant colonial activities. This series is a collaborative venture between the Cambridge Library Collection and the Royal Asiatic Society of Great Britain and Ireland, founded in 1823. The series reissues works from the Royal Asiatic Society's extensive library of rare books and sponsored publications that shed light on eighteenth- and nineteenth-century European responses to the cultures of the Middle East and Asia. The selection covers Asian languages, literature, religions, philosophy, historiography, law, mathematics and science, as studied and translated by Europeans and presented for Western readers.

Life of Edward William Lane

The orientalist Edward William Lane (1801–1876) is best remembered for his mighty *Arabic–English Lexicon* and his classic translation of *One Thousand and One Nights*. Fascinated by Egypt, he made his first visit in 1825, undertaking a study of Egyptian life and customs which became his *Description of Egypt*, unpublished until more than a century after his death. His two-volume *Modern Egyptians* (also reissued in this series) remains an important text today. Material for the lexicon was collected in Cairo between 1842 and 1849 and, upon returning to England, Lane became a virtual recluse while compiling it. Following his death, the publication of the last three volumes was supervised by his great-nephew Stanley Lane-Poole (1854–1931). The sixth was prefaced with this biographical account, first published separately in 1877. It is based upon family recollections, the manuscript of *Description of Egypt*, and Lane's diary of his second stay there.

T0345390

Cambridge University Press has long been a pioneer in the reissuing of out-of-print titles from its own backlist, producing digital reprints of books that are still sought after by scholars and students but could not be reprinted economically using traditional technology. The Cambridge Library Collection extends this activity to a wider range of books which are still of importance to researchers and professionals, either for the source material they contain, or as landmarks in the history of their academic discipline.

Drawing from the world-renowned collections in the Cambridge University Library and other partner libraries, and guided by the advice of experts in each subject area, Cambridge University Press is using state-of-the-art scanning machines in its own Printing House to capture the content of each book selected for inclusion. The files are processed to give a consistently clear, crisp image, and the books finished to the high quality standard for which the Press is recognised around the world. The latest print-on-demand technology ensures that the books will remain available indefinitely, and that orders for single or multiple copies can quickly be supplied.

The Cambridge Library Collection brings back to life books of enduring scholarly value (including out-of-copyright works originally issued by other publishers) across a wide range of disciplines in the humanities and social sciences and in science and technology.

Life of
Edward William Lane

STANLEY LANE-POOLE

CAMBRIDGE
UNIVERSITY PRESS

CAMBRIDGE UNIVERSITY PRESS

Cambridge, New York, Melbourne, Madrid, Cape Town,
Singapore, São Paolo, Delhi, Mexico City

Published in the United States of America by Cambridge University Press, New York

www.cambridge.org
Information on this title: www.cambridge.org/9781108055925

© in this compilation Cambridge University Press 2013

This edition first published 1877
This digitally printed version 2013

ISBN 978-1-108-05592-5 Paperback

LIFE

OF

EDWARD WILLIAM LANE.

LIFE

OF

EDWARD WILLIAM LANE,

HON. DOCTOR OF LITERATURE, LEYDEN ;
CORRESPONDENT OF THE INSTITUTE OF FRANCE ;
HON. MEMBER OF THE GERMAN ORIENTAL SOCIETY, THE ROYAL ASIATIC SOCIETY,
THE ROYAL SOCIETY OF LITERATURE, ETC. ;
AUTHOR OF "THE MODERN EGYPTIANS," AND "AN ARABIC-ENGLISH LEXICON" ;
TRANSLATOR OF "THE THOUSAND AND ONE NIGHTS"; ETC.

BY

STANLEY LANE POOLE.

———◆———

WILLIAMS AND NORGATE,

14, HENRIETTA STREET, COVENT GARDEN, LONDON ;
AND 20, SOUTH FREDERICK STREET, EDINBURGH.

—

1877.

LONDON :
GILBERT AND RIVINGTON, PRINTERS,
ST. JOHN'S SQUARE.

PREFACE.

In editing the Sixth Part of my Great-Uncle's Arabic Lexicon I thought it well to prefix to it a memoir of the author. From this the present edition is reprinted, with only a few verbal changes.

I have had to tell the story of a life spent, partly on account of ill health, but mainly for the sake of work, in seclusion. Few men knew Mr. Lane personally in his later years, and as time went on and the improbability of his living to finish his work became more and more apparent, his unwillingness to see anyone beyond his family circle and a few special friends became stronger than ever. Thus I have had no assistance from the recollections of friends. Nor have I derived the smallest help from letters. Mr. Lane had a deeply-rooted objection to the publication of letters meant only for private friends, and he unfortunately took care to have all his own letters from Egypt destroyed; whilst after his return to England he hardly ever wrote one except on questions of scholarship which he was asked to decide.

The only materials I have been able to make use of are the MS. of the "Description of Egypt," which tells something of Mr. Lane's first visit to the East; certain note-books kept by him during his first and second residences in Egypt; his published works ; and his sister's journal, kept during the third visit to Egypt. I have also been aided by the recollections of those near relations who constantly lived with him; whilst for the last ten years I can write from my own intimate association with my Great-Uncle.

The diary of Mr. Lane's second visit to Egypt I have reproduced almost entire. As the daily jotting-down of what he called his "idle moments" it reveals something of himself, and as the record of the changes which nearly ten years had brought about in the country, it will be acceptable to students of the history of the Europeanising movement in Egypt.

STANLEY LANE POOLE.

September, 1877.

1801—1876.

EDWARD WILLIAM LANE.

1801—1825.

THE life of a great scholar should not be suffered
to pass away into forgetfulness. The Arabs have
indeed a proverb, 'He who has left works behind
him dies not': but although so long as there are
students of the life and the literature of the East,
the memory of Lane cannot die, the personality
of the great Orientalist is rigidly excluded from
his writings; they reveal almost nothing of himself. If to stimulate the endeavours of others
by the example of a chief of their kind, to
encourage fainter hearts by telling them of the
strength and devotion of a master, be one of the
ends of biography, this brief and inadequate
memoir of perhaps the truest and most earnest
student this century has seen will not be deemed
superfluous. As the record of half a hundred

B

years of ceaseless labour, crowned with a perfection of scholarship to which even Germany avowedly yields the palm of undisputed supremacy, the life of Lane must needs be written.

Edward William Lane was born at Hereford on September 17th, 1801. He was the third son of the Rev. Theophilus Lane, LL.D., a Prebendary of Hereford; and his mother was Sophia Gardiner, a niece of Gainsborough the Painter. At first his education was conducted by his father, after whose sudden death in 1814 he was placed successively at the grammar-schools of Bath and Hereford, where he distinguished himself by his unusual power of application and by an almost equal mastery of classics and mathematics. The latter formed his principal study, for his mind was bent upon taking a degree at Cambridge, and then entering the Church. This desire to devote himself to a religious profession may have had its origin in the training of his mother, under whose influence his education was completed. Mrs. Lane was a woman of no ordinary mould. Gifted with high intellectual powers, which she had spared no pains to cultivate, she possessed a strength and beauty of character that won not only admiration but affection from all who were privileged to know her. It is easy to understand how great and how good must have been the influence of such a mother upon Edward Lane. He was wont to say that he owed his success in life to her teaching, and the saying, characteristic in its modesty, was doubtless partly true. His succéss was the result as much of character as of intellect.

The Cambridge project was never carried out. Lane indeed visited the university, but did not enter his name on the books of any college. A few days' experience of university life as it was in the first quarter of this century was sufficient to show him that in living in such society as he was then introduced to, and in conforming to its ways, he would be sacrificing what was to him dearer than all academic distinctions. That his mathematical training had been thorough is shown by the fact that immediately after giving up the idea of Cambridge, Lane procured a copy of the honour papers of the year and discovered that he could without difficulty solve every problem save

B 2

one ; and, as he has often told me, going to bed weary with puzzling out this single stumbling-block, he successfully overcame it in his sleep and, suddenly waking up, lit his candle in the middle of the night and wrote out the answer without hesitation.

The plan of Cambridge, and with it the Church, being given up, and his later training being too exclusively mathematical for him to think of Oxford, Lane joined his elder brother Richard (afterwards renowned for his skill in lithography, which was recognized by the Royal Academy in the election to an associateship) in London, where he spent some time in engraving. Although this profession was also shortly abandonèd, the years devoted to it were not thrown away. The taste for art which he had inherited with the Gains-borough blood and which his mother, who had spent a great part of her girlhood in her uncle's studio, spared no endeavour to foster, aided by the mechanical training of the graver, was afterwards turned to admirable results in Egypt. Side by side with his engraving, however, was the growing passion for Eastern things. Lane could not by his nature be idle for a moment, and the hours unfilled by his art were given up to hard reading. To such an extent was this zeal for study carried, that he began to grudge the necessary time for food and exercise. The result of inattention to the ordinary rules of health was a state of weakness that could offer but a faint resistance to the attack of typhus fever which now assailed him. With difficulty escaping with his life, he found his health unequal to the sedentary habits of the engraver. A man who was so weak, partly from the exhaustion of chronic bronchitis, and partly from the effects of the fever, that he sometimes could not walk along a street without clinging for support, was not fit to bend over copper-plate all day. He therefore determined to adopt some other way of life.

As early as 1822, Eastern studies had more than merely attracted Lane's interest. A manuscript grammar of colloquial Arabic in his handwriting bears this date: and he must have been studying some time before he could attempt a grammar of Arabic, even though it is only an abridgement of other works. From this year or earlier dates that severe devotion to the language and character of the Arabs which for more than half a century filled every moment of his studious life.

It was this taste for Oriental matters, seconded by his weak health, which could ill withstand a northern winter, that determined Lane to visit Egypt. Another motive may have been the hope of a post in the service of the British Government, which, he was informed by those who were qualified to speak, he stood a good chance of obtaining if he made himself well acquainted with Easterns at home. Whatever the motives, in 1825 Lane left England for the first of his three visits to the land of the Pharaohs.

1825—1828.

THE FIRST VISIT TO EGYPT.

THE "DESCRIPTION OF EGYPT."

ON Monday the 18th July 1825 Lane embarked on board the brig "Findlay," 212 tons, bound for Alexandria, and on the 24th he lost sight of the coast of England. The voyage, which occupied two months, was not altogether uneventful. On the 2nd September the "Findlay" nearly foundered in a hurricane off Tunis. The master seems to have been an incapable person, and no one else of the crew understood navigation. The night was starless; the sea ran so high that the heavy storm-compass in the binnacle could not traverse and was unshipped at every lurch; and, driven along between a lee shore and a dangerous reef, without compass, and the main

topmast carried away, the ship seemed doomed to
destruction.   It was at this critical moment that
the captain entreated Lane to take the helm.
Fortunately navigation had formed part of his
mathematical studies : but he was little more
than a boy and this was his first voyage ; he
might well have shrunk from the responsibility.
But he went at once to the wheel, where he had
to be lashed, or he had been washed overboard
by the seas that swept momently over the deck.
He had noticed the bearings of the lightning,
and by the flashes he steered. At last the
moon rose, and by her light the wreck was
cleared away and steering was less hazardous.
As day dawned the wind abated, and Lane
was able to bring the ship safely into Malta
harbour on the morning of the 4th.   Here she
remained six days for repair; and meanwhile
the crew mutinied, seemingly not without reason;
and Lane was aroused one morning with a shot
through his pillow.   He had come prepared for
dangers in Egypt, and these accidents by the
way did not discompose him.   On Monday the
19th September the shores of the Delta came in

sight: first the ruined tower of Aboo-Seer rose above the horizon; then "a tall distant sail," which proved to be the Great Pillar of Alexandria; then high hills of rubbish, crowned with forts; and at last the ships in the Old Harbour. The "Findlay" was ordered to enter the New Harbour, and there cast anchor in the midst of a shoal of Rosetta boats.

Although it was late in the afternoon and little could be seen before dark, Lane was too impatient to wait for the next day. He landed filled with profound emotion, feeling, he writes, like an Eastern bridegroom about to lift the veil of his as yet unseen bride. For his was not the case of an ordinary traveller. "I was not visiting Egypt merely for my amusement; to examine its pyramids and temples and grottoes, and after satisfying my curiosity to quit it for other scenes and other pleasures: but I was about to throw myself entirely among strangers, among a people of whom I had heard the most contradictory accounts; I was to adopt their language, their customs, and their dress; and in order to make as much progress as possible in the study of their literature, it was my intention to associate almost exclusively with the Muslim inhabitants."

The first sight that met his eye was singularly impressive. It was the time of afternoon prayers, and the chant of the Muëddin had just ceased as they landed. Muslims were performing the ablutions at the sea, or, this done, were praying on the beach, with that solemn gravity and with those picturesque and striking attitudes which command the respect of all standers-by. Lane always felt a strong veneration for a Muslim at his prayers, and it was a singularly auspicious moment for an enthusiastic Englishman to set foot on the Egyptian soil. As he walked on, till he reached one of the principal streets, his delight and wonder grew at every step. The peculiar appearance of the narrow street and its shops, the crowded passengers of every nation bordering on the Mediterranean, the variety of costume and countenance, the "bearded visage of the Turk, the Moor, and the Egyptian,—the noble and hardy look of the sunburnt Bedawee enveloped in his ample woollen sheet or hooded cloak,—the

mean and ragged clothing of many of the lower
orders, contrasted with the gaudy splendour
or graceful habit of some of their superiors,
—the lounging soldier with his pipe and pistols
and yataghán,—the blind beggar,—the dirty
naked child, and the veiled female," afforded
a picture beyond even what his dreams of
the land of the Arabian Nights had conjured
up. It is true the shady side of the scene was
somewhat forcibly disclosed a few paces further on, by a brawl, a murder, and a decapitation,
all occurring in the space of a few minutes
before the eyes of the young traveller. And
as he examined Alexandria at leisure, he began
to feel disappointed with it, and to long for Cairo.
Notwithstanding the characteristic sights that
first greeted him, the city was not Eastern enough,
and he would have found his stay there wearisome but for the kindness and hospitality of
Mr. Salt, the British Consul-General, who
received him like an old friend, although they
were strangers to each other, and gave him
a room in his country-house near the Báb-es-Sidr.
Lane found a " delightful retreat " in Mr. Salt's

garden, and plenty of entertainment in the company that visited the Consul. One of these friends, M. Linant, the indefatigable cartographer of Egypt, proposed that Lane should join his party to Cairo, an offer which, as a stranger and as yet unprovided with a servant, he gladly accepted.

On the 28th September the Reyyis and crew chanted the Fát'hah, the beautiful prayer which opens the Kur-án, and M. Linant and his party, accompanied by Lane, set sail on the Mahmoodeeyeh canal for the El-Káhirah "the Guarded." The voyage was in no wise remarkable. Lane made his usual careful notes of every thing he saw, from the saráb to the creaking of the sákiyehs and the croaking of the frogs. He described each village or town he passed, and observed the ways of the people working on shore or bathing in the Nile; and watched the simple habits of the boatmen, when the boat was made fast and their day's work was over, grouped round the fire on the bank, smoking and singing, and blowing their terrible double-pipes and making night hideous with their national drums;

and then contentedly spreading their mats, and, despising pillow and covering, falling happily asleep. On the 2nd October Lane had his first distant and hazy view of the Pyramids, and about five o'clock the boat was moored at Boolák, the port of Cairo, and the Reyyis thanked God for their safe arrival—"El-ḥamdu li-lláh bi-s-selámeh."

They rode at once to the city to tell the Vice-Consul of their arrival, that rooms might be made ready for them in Mr. Salt's house.

The first view of Cairo delighted Lane even more than he had expected, and here at least, where all was thoroughly Eastern and on a grand scale, no after disappointment could be expected. When he saw the numberless minarets towering above the wilderness of flat-roofed houses, and in turn crowned by the citadel, with the yellow ridge of El-Mukattam in the back-ground, Lane took heart again and rejoiced in the prospect of his future home. The next day he took up his quarters at the Consulate, abandoned his English dress and adopted the Turkish costume, and set out to look for a house. He soon found one near the Báb-el-Hadeed, belonging to 'Osmán, a Scotsman in the employ of the British Consul, who proved a very useful neighbour and a faithful friend. The furniture, after the usual native pattern, always a simple affair in the East, was quickly procured and the house was soon ready for his reception.

These matters took up the first five days in Cairo: but on the 8th October, every thing being in a fair way to completion at the house, a small party of Europeans, with Lane among them, made an excursion to the Pyramids. It was only a flying visit, to take the edge off his ardent curiosity, for he meant to go again and make careful drawings and measurements. He explored the Great Pyramid, and then in the night climbed to its summit and enjoyed a sight such as one hardly sees twice in a lifetime. The cold wind sweeping up the sides, with a sound like the roar of a distant cataract, echoed the weird feeling of the place and the time, with which the vaguely vast outline of the Second Pyramid, faintly discernable, and the wild figures of the Bedawee guides were in full harmony. Then the moon rose and lighted up the eastern side of the nearer pyramid with a magic effect. Two hours more and the sun had revealed the plain of Egypt, and Lane had been already amply rewarded for the dangers and trouble of his journey from England by one of the most wonderful views in the world.

After two months spent in Cairo, in the study of the people and their language, and in seeing the thousand beautiful things that the most picturesque of cities could then show, Lane again visited the Pyramids, this time for a fortnight, armed with stores and necessaries for living, and with materials for drawing and surveying, above all the camera lucida, with which all his drawings were made.

He took up his abode in a tomb of an unusually luxurious kind. It had three holes for windows, and was altogether about eight feet wide by twice as long, with a partition wall in the middle. Before the door was the usual accumulation of bones and rags, and even whole bodies of mummies : but the contemplation of these details gave Lane no

unpleasant sensations; he merely observed that
the skulls were extraordinarily thick.   Into
this cheerful habitation the baggage was carried, and though at first the interior looked
"rather gloomy," when "the floor was swept,
and a mat, rug, and mattress spread in the
inner apartment, a candle lighted, as well as
my pipe, and my arms hung about upon
wooden pegs driven into crevices in the wall,"
—the paintings had been effaced long before,
—" I looked around me with complacency, and
felt perfectly satisfied."   He was waited on
by his two servants, an Egyptian and a Nubian, whom he had brought from Cairo, and at
the door were two Arabs hired from the neighbouring village to guard against passing Bedawees.   All day long he was engaged in drawing
and describing and making plans; and then
in the evening he would come out on the
terrace in front of the tomb, and sit in the
shade of the rock (at Christmastide), drinking
his coffee and smoking his long chibook, and
"enjoying the mild air and the delightful view
over the plain towards the capital."

"In this tomb I took up my abode for a fortnight, and never did I spend a more happy time, though provided with fewer articles of luxury than I might easily and reasonably have procured. My appearance corresponded with my mode of living; for on account of my being exposed to considerable changes of atmospheric temperature in passing in and out of the Great Pyramid, I assumed the Hirám (or woollen sheet) of the Bedawee, which is a most convenient dress under such circumstances; a part or the whole being thrown about the person according to the different degrees of warmth which he may require. I also began to accustom myself to lay aside my shoes on many occasions, for the sake of greater facility in climbing and descending the steep and smooth passages of the pyramid, and would advise others to do the same. Once or twice my feet were slightly lacerated; but after two or three days they were proof against the sharpest stones. From the neighbouring villages I procured all that I wanted in the way of food; as eggs, milk, butter, fowls, and camels' flesh; but bread was not to be

c

obtained anywhere nearer than the town of
El-Geezeh, without employing a person to make
it.   One family, consisting of a little old man
named 'Alee, his wife (who was not half his
equal in years), and a little daughter, occupied
a neighbouring grotto, guarding some antiqui-
ties deposited there by Caviglia.   Besides these
I had no nearer neighbours than the inhabitants
of a village about a mile distant."   The solitude,
however, was broken two days after his arrival
by the appearance of a young Bedawee, who
frankly confessed he had deserted from the
Páshà's army and could not enter the villages,
and claimed Lane's hospitality, which was of
course immediately granted.   The young fellow
used to amuse his host in the evening, while he
smoked his pipe, by telling the famous stories
from the romance of Aboo-Zeyd, all the while
exciting the indignation of the Egyptian servant
by his contempt for the Felláheen.   He stayed
till Lane left, and when the latter asked him
where he would find protection now, he replied
with characteristic reliance upon providence,
" Who brought *you* here ?"

After a fortnight in his tomb at the Pyramids of El-Geezeh, spent in making drawings and plans of the pyramids and the surrounding tombs, Lane returned to Cairo on New Year's Eve. Here for two months and a half he devoted himself to the study of the "Mother of the World" and her inhabitants. Already possessed of an accurate knowledge of the modern Arabic language; being conformed to the customs of the people in all such external matters as dress and manners and outward habit of life; and being of that calm and self possessed nature absolutely necessary to one who would be intimate with Easterns, and moreover of a cast of countenance resembling so closely that of a pure Arab family of Mekkeh that an Egyptian, though repeatedly assured of the mistake, persisted in his belief that the reputed Ingleezee was a member of that family; Lane was able, as scarcely one other European has been, to mix among the people of Cairo as one of themselves, and to acquire not only the refinements of their idiomatic speech and the minute details of their etiquette, but also a perfect insight into their

habits of mind and ways of thought. The
Spirit of the East is a sealed book to ninety-
nine out of every hundred orientalists. To Lane
it was transparent. He knew the inner manners
of the Egyptian's mind as well as those of his
outer life. And this was the result of the many
years he lived among the people of Cairo, of
which these few months in 1826 were the beginning.

His life at this time, however, was not wholly
spent among Easterns. There was still a European side. He was one of the brilliant group of
discoverers who were then in Egypt : and young
as he was he was received among them with
cordial welcome and unfeigned appreciation.
Within the charmed circle to which Lane was
now admitted were men such as Wilkinson and
James Burton (afterwards Haliburton), the hiero-
glyphic scholars; Linant and Bonomi; the
travellers Humphreys, Hay, and Fox-Strang-
ways; the accomplished Major Felix, and his
distinguished friend Lord Prudhoe, of whose
noble appreciation of Lane's work much will
presently be said. With such friends and in

such a city as Cairo, the life of the young orientalist must have been enviable.

But the time had now come for the first Nile-voyage. The journey from Alexandria to Cairo had not damped the enthusiastic longing with which Lane looked forward to the upper country—Thebes and Philae and Dendarah. He determined to ascend to the Second Cataract, a limit further than most travellers then ventured and beyond which travelling was almost impossible. In March 1826 he hired a boat, for twenty-five dollars a month, manned by a crew of eight men, who were to find their own provisions, and on the 15th he embarked, set his cabin in order and sailed.

Lane's plan was, in the up-voyage to see in a cursory manner everything that could be seen, and in the down-voyage to make the notes and drawings from which he intended to construct his "Description of Egypt." In the up-voyage we see him sailing from one place of interest to another, with as little delay as possible; spending the whole day in walking to some ruin at a distance from the bank, and

the next day, and every day, so long as there
was anything worth visiting on shore. As a
sightseer in Egypt Lane was indefatigable. He
would walk on the hot plain, with the thermometer at 112° in the shade, till his feet were
blistered, and he had to throw himself on his
back to relieve them from the burning of the
sand. When there was nothing to take him on
shore, he would smoke his pipe on deck, and
watch the people in the villages as he passed,
or rest his eyes on the long lines of palms
and dom and nabk trees that fringe the bank.
Sometimes a compulsory variety was made by
the wind dropping, when the boatmen would
turn out and drag the tow-rope. Or the boat
was kept for days in an uninteresting place
by a wind against which towing was vain labour.
A sandstorm would now and then cause an
unpleasant diversion, and not only keep Lane
in his cabin, but follow him there and fill every
crevice. It was quite another matter, though,
with the sand-pillar; which was the work of an
'Efreet, who stirred up the dust in his flight,
and, being an 'Efreet, might be amenable to

persuasion. Lane encountered one of these pillars of sand in one of his walks, and following the instructions of his guide he accosted the 'Efreet with the cry of "Ḥadeed" ("iron"), and the sprite passed at a respectful distance. The modern life of Egypt claimed the traveller's attention no less than the ancient. He visited the tombs of the Sheykh El-Ḥareedee and the Sheykh 'Abd-el-Ḳádir El-Geelánee, and went through the usual ceremonies with a precision in which no Muslim could find a fault;- he received the calls of the various dignitaries on the way with the utmost courtesy, although he was obliged to decline the presents of Abyssinian girls and nargeelehs which they were fond of offering; and he seldom missed an opportunity of strolling through an Arab town, or watching an encampment of Bedawees, and learning something more of the ways of the people.

At Dendarah, near the end of April, Lane met James Burton, and together they suffered from the Khamáseen winds, and found they could make no drawings nor leave their boats.

On the 6th of May the great Propylæum of Thebes came in view ; on the 15th at Philae, they found Linant, who had left Cairo a couple of days earlier.   After going on to Aboo-Simbel, and then to the Second Cataract, Lane turned his boat and prepared to descend the Nile. He seems to have spent his time during the whole of this return voyage in drawing and measuring and describing, often sitting under an almost vertical sun, his thermometer occasionally bursting at 150°, and with no other protection from the scorching heat than a single tarboosh.   At Philae he again found Linant, waiting for the rising of the river to pass the Cataract, and during the eight days they spent together there Strangways made his appearance, went to Wádee Ḥalfeh, and then came back to them; and in company with him Lane continued his way down the river.   Seventy-three days (July 30 to October 11, 1826) were spent at Thebes, where he met Hay, in making a minute survey of the tombs and temples.   Here he lived in three different houses.   The first was Yáni's house, among the

tombs on the western side; then he moved
to a ruined part of the first propylæum of
El-Ḳarnak; and for fifteen days he lived in
one of the Tombs of the Kings, for the sake
of its comparative coolness. In the former
abodes the thermometer ranged from 90° to
108° in the shade; but in the Tombs of the
Kings it did not rise above 87°.

Coming back to Cairo, Lane went among
the people as before, busy in preparing his
account of their manners and customs, and his
description of their city. After several months
thus spent, he again started for the Nile, again
ascended to the Second Cataract, and stayed
forty-one days (November 1 to December 12,
1827) at Thebes, completing his survey of the
temples. And, having accomplished the great
object of his travels, having prepared a complete
description of Egypt and Lower Nubia, the
country and the monuments and the people,
he came back to Cairo in the beginning of
1828, and after a short stay at the capital,
and a final visit in the spring to the Pyramids of El-Geezeh and Saḳḳarah, in company

with Hay, he returned to England in the autumn of the year.

These three years of the first visit to Egypt had not been years of idleness. Lane was not the typical traveller, who travels for amusement, and perhaps writes a book to record his sensations for the gratification of an admiring public. Lane's object was a far different one. He travelled, so to say, to map the country. And his was a propitious time. Egypt had but recently been opened up to explorers, and no one had yet fully taken stock of her treasures. Hamilton, indeed, and Niebuhr had broken the ground with their books; but no systematic account of the country, its natural characteristics, its people, and its monuments, had yet been attempted. Successfully to perform such a work demanded long and unceasing labour and considerable abilities. Lane never shrank from toil of any kind, and he possessed just those natural gifts which were needed by one who should do this work. Lord Brougham once said, " I wonder if that man knows what his *forte* is ?—Description:" and Brougham was right. Very few men have possessed in an equal degree the power of minutely describing a scene or a monument, so that the pencil might almost restore it without a fault after the lapse of years. This power is eminently shown in the "Description of Egypt." Every temple or tomb, every village, every natural feature of the country, is described in a manner that permits no improving. The objects stand before you as you read, and this not by the use of imaginative language, but by the plain simple description. Lane had a vehement hatred of "fine writing," and often expressed his dislike to those authors who are credited with the habit of sacrificing the truth of their statements to the fall of the sentence. He always maintained that the first thing was to find the right word to express your meaning, and then to let the sentence fall as it pleased. It is possible that in his earliest work he carried this principle a little too far; and in his most finished production, the notes to "The Thousand and One Nights," considerable care may be detected in the composition. But in every thing he wrote, the prominent characteristic was perfect clearness, and nowhere is this more conspicuous than in the "Description of Egypt." But further, to prevent the scant possibility of mistaking the words, the work was illustrated by 101 sepia drawings, made with the camera lucida, (the invention of his friend Dr. Wollaston,) and therefore as exact as photography could make them, and far more pleasing to the eye. Those whose function it is to criticise artistic productions have unanimously expressed their admiration of these drawings. And though Lane would always say that the credit belonged to his instrument and not to himself, it is easy to see that they are the work of a fine pencil-hand, and could not have been done by any one who chose to look through a camera lucida. Altogether, both in drawings and descriptions, the book is unique of its kind.

It has never been published. And the reason is easily seen in the expense of reproducing the drawings. Lane himself was never a rich man, and could not have issued the book at his own expense, and no publisher was found sufficiently enterprising to risk the first outlay.

An eminent firm, indeed, accepted the work with enthusiasm, but subsequently retracted from its engagement in consequence of the paralysis of trade which accompanied the excitement of the Reform agitation. It is needless, however, to refer to affairs that happened nearly fifty years ago, although they were a cause of much annoyance and disappointment to the author of the "Description of Egypt"; who naturally was illdisposed to see the work of several years wasted, and who could not forget the high praises that had been passed upon the book and the drawings by all who were competent to form an opinion. There can be no doubt in the mind of any one who has studied the manuscript and the drawings, that travellers in Egypt have sustained in this work a loss which has not yet been filled up, and is not likely to be, unless the "Description of Egypt" should yet be published.

We have seen Lane in a phase of his life distinct from all the remainder. The years 1825—28 are the only time in which he could be called a traveller. Even then the traveller bent on the enjoyment of the wonders of a new land is swallowed up in the student intent on understanding the monuments of a marvellous antiquity. But after this first visit all traces of the traveller disappear, and the serious laborious student becomes everything. Once again in after years did Lane ascend the Nile as far as Thebes, and live the old life in his tomb; but it was to avoid the Plague, and his visit there was still devoted to study. Henceforward we shall see, not the enterprising and often daring explorer, climbing flat-faced cliffs, swinging down a mummy-pit, crawling in the low passages of tombs and pyramids, but a scholar at his desk, a learned man honoured in learned circles, the highest authority on matters Arabian to whom England or Europe could appeal.

THE SECOND VISIT TO EGYPT (1833—5.)

FOR some time after his return to England, Lane was occupied in working his Egyptian notes and diaries into the form that the manuscript of the "Description of Egypt" now wears. It has already been said that the negotiations with the publishers for the production of the book fell to the ground. But before this happened, Lane had separated from the body of the work his account of the modern inhabitants of Egypt, which it was thought would appear to greater advantage and be more widely read as a distinct book. This part of the "Description" was shown to Lord Brougham, who at once recognised its high merit, and recommended it to the Society for the Diffusion of Useful Knowledge, of which he was a Member of Committee. It was in

consequence of the acceptance of the work by
the Society that Lane determined to visit
Egypt again, in order to enlarge and perfect his
account of the people. This is an instance of
that thoroughness which is shown in every work
of his. Whatever came to his hand to do, he
did it with all his might. He would never
condescend to anything approaching slovenly
work; and thought little of crossing the Mediterranean and staying two years at Cairo in order
to bring nearer to perfection a sketch of the
manners and customs of the inhabitants of Egypt,
which to an ordinary writer would have seemed
to stand in need of no revision. Without hesitation he went over the whole ground again,
verified each statement, and added much that
had been omitted from the earlier and more
concise work. During the two years he spent
in the Egyptian metropolis, scarcely a day passed
without his going out among his Muslim friends
and accustoming himself more completely to their
manners, or witnessing the various public festivals
of the year. Every day's experience was carefully
recorded in a little library of note-books, all

written in his singularly clear and neat hand,
except where here and there an Egyptian friend
has scribbled his own statement in Arabic. One
of these note-books appears to have been kept for
recording the more important scenes that Lane
witnessed, and is fortunately dated, so as to
form an intermittent diary. As this is the
only journal he ever kept, to my knowledge,
except a brief account of his first Nile-voyage,
it is here reproduced. Besides the necessary
suppression of a few sentences relating to family
matters, certain long passages have been omitted,
since they occur verbatim in Lane's published
works. It is not often that the pages of a
diary can be transferred to a finished book
like "The Modern Egyptians" without even
verbal alteration. But it was the same with
everything Lane wrote. If he was asked a
question by letter, his answer was always fit
for publication, both in style and in accuracy
of matter.

———

London, 25th Oct., 1833.—Engaged my passage to
Alexandria on board the merchant brig Rapid, Capt.
Phillips, 162 tons, for 30 guineas, to be found with all

necessary stores, poultry, &c.—6th Nov. Embarked at St. Katharine's Dock.—7th. Sailed.—25th. Passed Gibraltar.—5th Dec. Passed Malta.—13th (1st of Shaabán, 1249). Arrived at Alexandria.

It had rained almost incessantly, and very heavily, during the three nights previous to our arrival at Alexandria; and the streets were consequently in a most filthy state. The general appearance of the people was also far more miserable than when I was here before. The muddy state of the streets doubtless confined most well-dressed persons to their houses; but it is rather to the severe oppression of late years, and to repeated conscriptions, which have deprived many parents of the support they received from the labour of their sons, that I attribute the difference which I remarked in the general aspect of the population of this place. A few days before my arrival, some persons from Constantinople had brought the plague there. They were put into quarantine; and the disease had thus been confined within the Lazarette, which was surrounded by a cordon of soldiers. There had been 87 cases, and 23 deaths.—I dined and slept at Mr. Harris's country-house, which is in an angle of the garden in which the house that Mr. Salt resided in is situated, where I stayed during my first visit to Alexandria. A part of this garden is converted into a burial-place for the English. Mr. Salt is buried there.— Alexandria is rapidly increasing towards the site of the old city: several large and handsome buildings have lately been erected in that quarter.

14th. Removed my luggage from the brig to a boat

on the Maḥmoodeeyeh; and in the afternoon set sail
for the Nile. Paid 45 piasters for the voyage to the
Nile.—15th. Arrived before sunrise at the Foom, or
the mouth of the canal, where it communicates with the
Nile. A bridge with gates has lately been constructed
across the mouth, to retain the water in the canal during
the season of low Nile.—I here had to engage another
boat, on the Nile. Bargained for 80 piasters for the
voyage to Maṣr (or Cairo). Proceeded to Fooweh; but
could not continue our voyage in consequence of a violent
contrary wind. The air was very thick; and I could hardly
fancy myself in Egypt. The river still very turbid. There
were many boats here conveying Turkish pilgrims on
their way to join the Egyptian Caravan to Mekkeh.
Fooweh seems to be falling to utter ruin and to be inhabited by the most squalid miserable people I ever
beheld. I am told that I shall remark the same at all
the villages we have to pass; and the reason is this:—all
the best-looking young men have been picked for the army
or navy, and their wives and lovers have mostly followed
them; but being parted from them on their arrival at
the metropolis have there betaken themselves to prosti-
tution; and Maṣr now absolutely swarms with prostitutes.
Thus the villages have been half desolated; and seem to
be peopled in general with the most wretched, ugly, old,
and haggard paupers. I see scarcely one good-looking
young woman among a hundred; or scarcely one where
I used to see a score; and almost all are in rags.—16th.
In the afternoon, though the wind was still very high
and from the S.W., we proceeded. Stopped for the

night under the west bank, a little below Shubra Kheet. Several heavy showers of rain fell, accompanied with violent gusts of wind, which obliged many boats, loaded with Turkish pilgrims, to stop at the same part. From a boat next above ours, during a shower of rain, there poured forth a number of these pilgrims, each with his ewer in his hand, to perform the ablution preparatory to prayer; and some of them aged and decrepit. While meditating on their zeal and the hardships which awaited them and admiring their grave and venerable aspect, I was surprised to see six of them, and among these some of the most aged, run to a táboot (a kind of water-wheel used for irrigation), and, with shouts such as their children would have used on a similar occasion, amuse themselves by exerting what little strength they had to perform, all the six together, the work of one cow; and turn, which they could only do very slowly, the stiff and creaking wheel. A few minutes after, they performed their devotions, all of them together, with the utmost solemnity and decorum, ranged in ranks, four abreast, under the partial shelter of some durah about 12 feet high: one acted as Imám, in the first rank; and having previously chanted the *adán*, recited the prayers, chanting the *fard*-prayers in a high key and loud voice.—To-day I began to feel the effect which is often produced by first drinking the water of the Nile, and by the cool air of the night; my cabin being only furnished with blinds, like those of an English carriage, to the windows, I was much exposed to the night-air. — 17th. Advanced to Shubra Kheet. The

weather being boisterous and rainy, and my reiyis determined to proceed, I made a new agreement with him; to
pay 20 piasters a day, and to stop when and where I
desired. Accordingly I remained the rest of this day,
and the following night, at Shubra Kheet.—18th. Of
the prudence of the new arrangement which I had made
for my boat I received a strong proof in information
brought me to-day that a boat which I had first hired
at the Foom, about the same size and on the same terms
as that in which I now am, but afterwards left for the
latter boat in consequence of an order that vessels there
should take their departure according to the order in
which they lay, had been capsized in the night: the crew
and passengers were saved; but remained shivering in
their wet clothes for many hours; no village being near.
Had this been my case, in my present indisposed state, I
should probably have lost my life; or, if not, my books
&c. would have been lost or spoiled. My informant
thanked God for my preservation; and I most heartily
joined him.—19th. Proceeded to Sháboor: the wind still
very violent and contrary: on the 20th, to Nádir; 21st,
to Záwiyet Razeem, by the tow-rope; having scarcely a
breath of wind.—22nd. Calm. Proceeded, by towing,
to Wardán.—23rd and 24th. As the wind was violent and
contrary during the greater part of each of these days, my
reiyis absented himself from the boat. I punish him by
deducting two days' pay.—25th. Arrived within five
miles of Boolák.

26th. Arrived at Boolák about noon. Sent for a jani-
sary from the Consulate to pass my luggage at the cus-

tom-house, and rode up to my old friend 'Osmán, who had made preparations for my reception in a house belonging to him and next to that in which he resides. This house I have engaged for the period of my intended stay in Maṣr. It is situated in the most healthy part of the town, near the N.W. angle; and to me, who have suffered from ophthalmia, it is a desirable residence, as it has glass windows. I have no doubt that ophthalmia in this country is generally the effect of suppressed perspiration, which is most commonly induced by the night-air (the windows of almost all the houses in Masr and the other towns being merely of wooden lattice-work); and that it is aggravated by the habit of keeping the head too warm, and the feet too cool.

The aspect of Maṣr, as seen in the approach from the port, has been much improved since the period of my last visit by the removal of many of the mounds of rubbish which rose along that side, and by most of the space which these unsightly objects occupied being converted into gardens. A short time ago, European travellers, if habited in the Turkish or Egyptian dress, were not allowed to enter the gates of Maṣr without a passport (called *tezkereh*), which was shown to the guard. This custom is now dispensed with. It was adopted in order to ascertain the number of the population; and to insure that no one of the natives might be unknown, and so escape paying the firdeh or poll-tax. In the interior of the metropolis I observe more ruined houses than when I was last here; and in the appearance of the lower orders, more wretchedness. No change has taken place

in the style of the costume of the natives; but the
military officers, and the Turks in the employ of the
Báshà, have adopted the Nizámee dress, which was becoming common among them before I last quitted Maṣr.
The head-dress (being merely a ṭarboosh, without the
muslin or Kishmeeree shawl wound round it) has lost its
elegance; and the whole dress is less becoming and graceful than the Memlook costume which it has superseded;
though it is more convenient for walking and any active
exertion. Formerly, a grandee of Maṣr, with his retinue
of twenty or more well-mounted men, clad in habits of
various and brilliant hues, and with splendid accoutre-
ments, the saddles covered with embroidered velvet and
plates of gilt and embossed silver, and the bridles,
headstalls, and other trappings ornamented in a similar
manner and with rows of gold coins suspended to them,
presented a strikingly picturesque and pompous spectacle.
Sights of this description are no longer witnessed in the
Egyptian metropolis. Even the Báshà, when he occasionally rides through the streets, is followed by only
three or four attendants, and is not more distinguished
by the habits than by the number of his retinue. As
dark colours, and particularly black, are now fashionable
among the Turks, and their dresses are generally embroidered with silk, instead of gold lace, there is much less
contrast and variety observable in the costumes of the
passengers in the crowded streets; but at present there
is a little more variety and bustle than is usual, from the
number of Turkish pilgrims resting here on their way to
Mekkeh.

My old acquaintance the sheykh Ahmad (or *seyd* Aḥmad, for he is a *shereef*) called on me as soon as he had heard of my arrival. He has resumed his old habit of visiting me almost every day; both for the sake of getting his dinner or supper, or at least tobacco and coffee, and to profit in his trade of bookseller. I wish I could make a portrait which would do justice to his singular physiognomy. For many years he has been nearly blind: one of his eyes is quite closed: the other is ornamented on particular occasions, as the two great festivals, &c., with a border of kohl; though he is a shocking sloven at all times. He tells me that he has taken a second wife, and a second house for her; but that he is as poor as ever; and that my usual yearly present of a dress will be very acceptable.*
He has a talent for intrigue and cheating, which he exercises on every opportunity; being lax in morals, and rather so in his religious tenets. Notwithstanding these defects, and sometimes in consequence of his having the latter defect, I find him very useful. Much of the information that I have obtained respecting the manners and customs of his countrymen has been derived from him, or through his assistance; as he scruples not to be communicative to me on subjects respecting which a bigoted Muslim would be silent. He has just brought me a *muṣḥaf* (or copy of the Ḳur-án), which he wishes me to purchase; but he thinks it necessary, as he did on former similar occasions, to offer some excuse for his doing so. He remarks that by my

---

* Here follows the story of Sheykh Aḥmad's mother, told in the preface to *The Modern Egyptians*, p. xviii. (5th Ed.)

following or conforming with many of the ceremonies of
the Muslims I tacitly profess myself to be one of them;
and it is incumbent on him to regard me in the most
favourable light. "You give me," says he, "the salutation
of 'Peace be on you!' and it would be impious in me, and
directly forbidden by my religion, to pronounce you an
unbeliever; for He whose name be exalted hath said in
the Excellent Book,—' Say not unto him who greeteth thee
with peace, Thou art not a believer' (ch. iv., v. 96) —
therefore," he adds, "it is no sin in me to put into your
hands the noble Ḳur-án: but there are some of your
countrymen who will take it in unclean hands, and even
put it under them and sit upon it! I beg God's forgiveness
for talking of such a thing: far be it from you to do so:
you, praise be to God, know and observe the command
' None shall touch it but those who are clean.'" (ch. lvi.,
v. 78: these words are often stamped upon the cover.) He
once sold a muṣhaf on my application to a countryman
of mine, who, being disturbed just as the bargain was
concluded by some person entering the room, hastily put
the sacred book on the deewán and under a part of his
dress, to conceal it: the bookseller was much scandalized
by this action; thinking that my friend was sitting upon
the book, and doing so to show his contempt of it. There
was only one thing that I had much difficulty in persuading
him to do, during my former visit to this country; which
was to go with me to the mosque of the Ḥasaneyn, the
burial-place of the head of the Prophet's grandson, El-
Ḥoseyn, and the most sacred of the mosques of Maṣr.
On passing with him before one of the entrances of this

building, one afternoon in Ramadán, when it was crowded
with Turks, and many of the principal people of the
metropolis were among the congregation, I thought it
a good opportunity to see it to the greatest advantage,
and asked my companion to go in with me. He positively
refused, in the fear of my being discovered to be an Englishman, which might so rouse the fanatic anger of some of
the Turks there as to expose me to some act of violence. I
therefore entered alone. He remained at the door; following me with his eye only (or his only eye), and wondering
at my audacity; but as soon as he saw me acquit myself
in the usual manner, by walking round the bronze screen
which surrounds the monument over the spot where the
martyr's head is buried and then going through the regular
attitudes of prayer, he came in and said his prayers by
my side.—The principal subjects of the conversations which
my other Masree acquaintances have held with me since
my return to their country have been the oppression which
they suffer under the present government, the monopolies
of the Báshà, and the consequent dulness of trade and
dearness of provisions, &c. The sheykh Ahmad is less
querulous: he praises the Báshà for including booksellers
among persons of literary and religious professions, from
whom no firdeh is exacted. He and another bookseller, who
is his superior, are agents for the sale of the books printed
at the Báshà's press, at Boolák. They have a shop in the
principal street of the city (nearly opposite the entrance to
Khán El-Khaleelee), which will be a convenient place for
me to repair to on the occasions of public processions.

Friday, 10th of January.—Last day (29th) of Shaabán.—

In the afternoon of this day I went to the booksellers'
shop to see the procession of the *Leylet er-Rooyeh*, or Night
of the Observation of the new moon of Ramadán, the month
of abstinence. Soon after the *'aṣr*, the shops were mostly
shut, and the *maṣṭabahs* occupied by spectators, old and
young. The foremost persons in the procession, a company
of Niẓám infantry, passed the place where I was sitting
(within ten minutes' walk of the Ḳádee's house, whither
they were destined) about an hour and a quarter before
sunset. The whole procession consisted of nothing more
than several companies of Niẓám troops, each company
preceded and followed by bearers of mesh'als, to light them
on their return, together with small parties of members of
those trades which furnish the metropolis with provisions:
a group of millers following one party of soldiers; a group
of bakers, another: after all of whom came the Moḥtesib,
with attendants. The soldiers were accompanied by drum-
mers and fifers, and one band. The members of trades who
took part in the procession, with several faḳeers, shouted
as they passed along—" *O ! Eṣ-ṣaláh ! Eṣ-ṣaláh ! Ṣalloo
'ala-n-Nebee ! 'aleyhi-s-selám !* " (O ! Blessing ! Blessing !
Bless ye the Prophet ! On him be peace !). After every
two or three companies there was an interval of many
minutes: so that about an hour elapsed before the procession had passed the place where I sat. After waiting some
time at the Ḳádee's, the information that the new moon
had been seen was brought there; and the soldiers and
other persons who had formed the procession thither divided
themselves into several companies, and perambulated different quarters of the town; shouting *Ya' ummata kheyri-l-*

ana'm! Siya'm! Siya'm! (O followers of the best of the
creation! Fasting! Fasting!). The mosques were all
illuminated within; and lamps hung at their entrances,
and upon the galleries of the mád'nehs.—When the moon
is not seen, the people are informed by the cry of *Ghadà
min shahri Shaqba'n! Fiṭár! Fiṭár!* (To-morrow is of
the month of Shaabán! No fasting! No fasting!).—The
people seem as merry to-night as they usually do when
released from the miseries of the day's fast.*

11th of January.—1st of Ramaḍán.—Instead of seeing,
as at other times, most of the passengers in the streets
with the pipe in the hand, we now see them empty-handed,
or carrying a stick or cane; but some of the Christians
are not afraid, as they used to be, of smoking in their
shops during this month. The streets in the morning have
a dull appearance, many of the shops being shût; but in
the afternoon they are as much crowded as usual, and all
the shops are open. A similar difference is also observable
in the manners and temper of the people during the day-
time and at night: while fasting, they are generally speak-
ing very morose: in the evening, after breakfast, they
are unusually affable and cheerful. As Ramaḍán now falls
in the winter, the fast is comparatively easy; the days
being short, and the weather cool: therefore thirst is
not felt so severely. The period from the commencement
of the fast (the *imsák*), which is at this season within two
hours of sunrise, to the time when it ends, or sunset, is
now (in the beginning of the month) 12 hours and

---

* Cp. *Mod. Eg.* p. 472.

12 minutes : at the end of the month it will be 12 hours
and 47 minutes. Servants who are fasting (as mine, and
most others, are), if they have to bring a pipe to a person
who is not keeping the fast, will not draw the smoke as
usual at other times, but put a live coal upon the tobacco,
and blow upon it, or wave the pipe through the air ; and
then present it. I take my principal meal now at sunset,
in order that it may serve as a breakfast to any friend who
may call on me in the evening, at or before that time.
Towards evening, and for some time after sunset, the beg-
gars in the streets are now more than usually importunate
and clamorous. I often hear the cries of *Fatooree 'aleyk
ya' Rabb!* (My breakfast must be thy gift, O Lord !)—
Ana deyf Allah wa-n-Nebee (I am the guest of God and
the Prophet !)—and the following, which exhibits a union
(not uncommon in similar cries) of the literary and popular
dialects of Arabic—*Men faṭṭar sa'im luh agrun da'im* (Who
gives breakfast to a faster will have an enduring recom-
pense). The coffee-shops are now much frequented by
persons of the lower orders ; many of whom prefer to break
their fast with a cup of coffee and a pipe. Parties assemble
at these shops a little before sunset, and wait there to hear
the evening call to prayer, which announces the termination
of the day's fast. Some of the coffee-shops offer the attraction of a reciter of tales, or poetical romances, during the
nights of Ramaḍán. It is also a custom among some of
the 'Ulamà of Maṣr to have a Zikr performed in their
houses, by a numerous company of faḳeers, every night
during this month.* My almost daily visiter, the sheykh

---

* Cp. *Mod. Eg.* pp. 474—6.

Ahmad, the bookseller, tells me that he cannot spend much
time with me this month; as he sleeps half the day, and
breakfasts, and takes part in a Zikr, every evening, at
the house of the late sheykh El-'Aroosee, who was one
of the four great sheykhs of Maṣr, presiding over the
Ḥanafeeyeh, of whom he was also the muftee.—As I
was sitting at the booksellers' shop to-day, the Báshà,
Moḥammad 'Alee, rode by, on his way to say the afternoon prayers in the mosque of the Ḥasaneyn, followed
by only four attendants; the first of whom bore his seg-
gádeh (or prayer-carpet), in an embroidered kerchief, on
his lap. The Báshà was very plainly dressed, with a white
turban. I should not have known him, had I not been
informed that it was he; for he appears much older than
when I was last in Egypt; though he looks remarkably
well. He saluted the people right and left as he passed
along: all rising to him.—It is the general fashion of the
principal Turks in Maṣr, and of many of their countrymen,
to repair to the mosque of the Ḥasaneyn in the afternoon
during Ramaḍán, to pray and lounge; and on these occasions, a number of Turkish tradesmen (called Toḥafgee-
yeh, or Toḥafjeeyeh) expose for sale, in the court of the
meyḍa-ah (or tank for ablution) of this mosque, a variety
of articles of taste and luxury suited to the wants of their
countrymen; such as porcelain, glass, gold, silver, brass,
and copper wares; cutlery; mouth-pieces of pipes and
pipe-sticks; and many other commodities, chiefly from
Constantinople, or other places in Europe. The interior of
the Ḥasaneyn during the afternoon in Ramaḍán is one
of the most interesting sights in Maṣr; but from the
circumstances which render it so, and particularly from

its being the most sacred of all the mosques in Maṣr,
none but a Muslim can enter and witness the scene
which it presents, unless accompanied by an officer of
the government, without imminent risk of being discovered, violently turned out, insulted with scurrilous
language, and perhaps beaten or spit upon. I only once
ventured into this mosque on such an occasion; and then
was careful to perform all the usual ceremonies. Many
persons go to the mosque of the Ḥasaneyn to offer up their
petitions for particular blessings, in the belief that the
sanctity of the place will ensure the success of their prayers.

A man was beheaded to-day, for stealing several pipes and
drinking-cups, belonging to the Báshà, in the Citadel.

Feb. 9th.—Last day (30th) of Ramaḍán.—Ramaḍán
has passed away with scarcely any incident to relieve its
dulness, excepting the usual merry-making of the lower
orders of the people at night in the coffee-shops, where
smoking tobacco or hemp, playing at some kind of game,
or listening to a story-teller, were their ordinary amuse-
ments. I have not observed funerals to be more numerous
than usual during the latter part of the month, as is
the case when Ramaḍán falls in the warmer seasons;
but the people have not seemed less out of humour with
the fast. Weariness and moroseness are the predominant
effects of the observance of Ramaḍán; and if people are
seen at this time more than usually occupied in mumbling
portions of the Ḳur-án, I think their motive is rather
to pass away the time than anything else. I am told that
many more persons break the fast now than did when
I was last here. Even the Ḳádee told an acquaintance

of mine, a few days ago, that it was his custom only to keep the first two and last two days of the fast. By the poor, in general, it is still rigidly kept; and, by them, most severely felt, as they can seldom relax from their ordinary labours. There is now living in this city an old man who fasts every day in the year, from day-break to sunset, excepting on the occasions of the two 'Eeds (or festivals), when it is unlawful for the Muslim to fast. At night he eats very sparingly. He keeps a shop in the shoe-market called Ḳasabat Rudwán, where he is generally seen occupied in reciting the Ḳur-án and handling his beads. It is said that there are several other persons here who fast in the same austere manner.—The weather during the month which is just expiring has been of an unusual kind: several very heavy showers of rain have fallen; and the streets have seldom been dry more than two or three days together.

In the afternoon of this day (at the hour of the *'asr*) the guns of the Citadel announced the termination of the period of the fast: the new moon having been seen. The fast is, however, kept till sunset. In the evening, the guns fired again. With sunset, the *'Eed* commences. The people are all rejoicing: swings and whirligigs are erected in many parts of the town, and in its environs; and several story-tellers and reciters of poetry have collected audiences in various places.

10th.—First day of the *'Eed*.—At day-break, all the mosques were crowded with worshippers, to perform the prayers of the 'Eed; and now, every minute, friends are seen in the streets congratulating, embracing, and kissing,

each other. Many of the people (all who can afford)
are seen in complete new suits of clothes: others, with
a new 'eree, or ṭarboosh and turban, or, at least, a new
pair of red or yellow shoes. Most of the shops are shut,
excepting those where eatables are sold. The people are
mostly occupied in visits of congratulation; or repairing,
particularly the women, to the tombs of their relatives.
Donkeys laden with palm-branches, for the visiters of
the tombs, obstruct the streets in many places. The guns
of the Citadel are fired at noon and in the afternoon (at
the *'aṣr*) on each of the three days of the 'Eed.

12th.—Last day of the 'Eed.—This day I accompanied
my neighbour 'Osmán to visit the tomb of the sheykh
Ibraheem (Burckhardt), in the cemetery of Báb en-Nasr,
on the north of the city, to see that the monument was in
good repair, and to pay to the memory of the lamented
traveller that tribute of respect which is customary on
the occasion of the 'Eed. The principal part of the burial-
ground, directly opposite the Báb en-Nasr, was occupied
by dense crowds of persons who had collected there for
their amusement, and presented a most singular scene.
Vast numbers of tents were erected; some, for the reception of idlers; but most, for the visiters of the tombs;
many of whom, conspicuous by their palm-branches, were,
like ourselves, making their way with much difficulty
through the multitude. A woman who had fallen down
here on the first day of the 'Eed was trodden to death.
Being mounted on donkeys, we got on better than some
others; but our palm-branch, borne before us, and showing our pious intention, had not the effect of inducing

E

any one to move out of our way. A large space was
occupied by swings and whirligigs, all in rapid motion,
and loaded with boys and girls : the principal objects of
attraction to persons of maturer age were conjurors, mu-
sicians, dancing-girls, and dancing-men. Having passed
through the most crowded part of the cemetery, we soon
arrived at the tomb of the sheykh Ibraheem. It is a plain
and humble monument of the usual oblong form, constructed of the common, coarse, calcareous stone of the
neighbouring mountain range of Muḳattam, with a stela
of the same stone, roughly cut, and without any inscrip-
tion, at the head and foot. Numerous faḳeers resort to
the cemeteries during the three days of the 'Eed, to perform, for the remuneration of a piaster or two, the service
usual on those occasions when visiters arrive; consisting
of the recital of, at least, one of the longer chapters of
the Ḳur-án, and afterwards of the Fát'ḥah, which latter
the visiters recite with him. One of them was employed
to perform this service by my friend. He did it very
rapidly, and without much reverence, seated at the foot
of the tomb. This being finished, and the palm-branch
broken in pieces and laid on the tomb, a fee was given to
the guardian of the tombs, and we returned.—'Osmán
performed the pilgrimage in company with the sheykh
Ibraheem. He presented me a few days ago with the
certificate of Ibraheem's pilgrimage. It is a paper of the
size of a small quarto leaf: the greater part occupied by a
representation of the temple of Mekkeh, drawn with ink,
and ornamented with red, yellow, and green, and with
silver leaf: beneath which picture is written the document

of which the following is a copy.—"Praise be to God,
who hath made the pilgrimage to be rightly accomplished,
and the intention rewarded, and sin forgiven. To proceed.
—The respected ḥágg Ibraheem hath performed the pilgrimage, according to the divine ordinances, and accomplished all the incumbent ordinances of the Prophet,
completely and perfectly. And God is the best of witnesses. The halt was on the 9th day of the month of
El-Ḥeggeh, in the year 1229."

15th.—Witnessed the procession of the Kisweh, which
I have described in one of my note-books.*

17th.—The Magician 'Abd El-Ḳádir came to me. His
performances unsuccessful.

18th.—A man was beheaded yesterday; and another
to-day. One was for entering a house to rob, and for at-
tempting to murder the owner. He locked the latter in
one of the rooms, and then proceeded to rifle the house.
On descending, he saw the owner at a window, calling for
assistance; and fired a pistol at him.—The crime of the
other, who was a Turk, a ḳowwás of the Báshà, was
robbing and murdering a Turkish pilgrim. He arrested
the pilgrim on the canal of Alexandria, under pretence
of his being required to answer some charge preferred
against him before Moḥarram Bey, the Governor of
Alexandria. After conducting him some little distance
towards Alexandria, he murdered him, and threw his
body into the pit of a sáḳiyeh. The companions of the
unfortunate man, some days after, being surprised at

---

* Cp. *Mod. Eg.* p. 480.

E 2

hearing no tidings of him, applied to Moḥarram Bey; and finding that he knew nothing of the circumstance, searched for and apprehended the murderer.—Robberies have become very frequent here of late: crime, as might be expected, increasing with the oppression and misery of the people.—News arrived to-day of a number of Aḥmad Báshà's horses having been stolen, by a party of Bedawees, from the Feiyoom, where they had been sent for the clover season.

20th.—The Magician came again, in the evening. His performances I have described in one of my note-books.*

27th.—Went to the Ḥasaneyn, to see the Kisweh, the Burḳo', &c., previously to their being packed up and dispatched with the caravan to Mekkeh. The sewing of the Kisweh was not quite completed: several men and women were at work upon it in the great hall, or portico. I asked for, and obtained, for a trifling present, a piece of the Kisweh, a span in length, and nearly the same in breadth. In sewing the several breadths together, it is necessary to cut off some small strips; and these are sold, or given, to persons who apply for them; being considered as amulets. In the saloon of the tomb, I found several pious visiters; and, among them, a poor man, standing before the bronze screen which surrounds the monument, and praying aloud, with uplifted hands, for food; saying—" Bread, O Lord! I pray for bread: I do not ask for dates: I only pray for bread."—After I had recited the Fát'hah, according to custom, at the shrine

---

* Cp. *Mod. Eg.* pp. 268, ff.

of Hoseyn, I went to a small apartment adjoining the mosque, in which were placed the Burko', the covering for the Makám Seydna Ibraheem, the covering of the Maḥmal (which were partly unfolded for me to see), the Ḥegáb (or Mushaf), of the Maḥmal, and the embroidered green silk bag in which is kept the key of the Kaạbeh. As soon as I had gratified my curiosity by inspecting these sacred objects, and again recited the Fát'hah, by desire of the persons who showed them to me, and who did the same, I was overwhelmed with applications for presents by about a dozen ministers and inferior servants of the mosque. Three or four piasters satisfied them; or at least silenced them.—On my way to the Ḥasaneyn, I passed through the great mosque El-Azhar. I was obliged to send my servant by another way because he was carrying my pipe, which could not with propriety be taken into the mosque, though several persons were carrying about bread and other eatables in the great court and in the place of prayer, for sale to the mugáwireen (or students) and the other numerous frequenters of this great temple and university. The weather being not warm, the court was crowded with groups of students and idlers, lounging or basking in the sun; and part of it was occupied by schoolmasters with their young pupils. The interior of this mosque always presents a very interesting scene, at least to me, from its being the principal centre of attraction to the votaries of religion, of literature, and of other sciences, throughout the Muslim world. The college has just been disgraced by one of its members

having been convicted of a robbery; and this morning
several of the learned community, having heard that
eight men were just about to be hanged, were in a state
of alarm lest their guilty associate should be one of that
number. A brother of this culprit was pointed out to me,
conversing, with apparent apathy, with another person,
who, turning to me, asked me if I knew of any case on
record of a member of the 'Ulamà being hanged.—
Shortly after I had quitted the Hasaneyn, the eight
men above-mentioned were hanged; each in a different
part of the town. The member of the college was not
among them. In crossing the principal street of the city,
I saw one of them, hanging at the window of a sebeel,
or public fountain. He was a soldier. His crime was
robbery and murder. Another of the eight was hanged
for a similar crime. He entered the house of a rich
Jewess, ostensibly for the purpose of taking away the
dust; murdered her, by cutting off her head; put her
remains into a large zeer (or water-jar), and having
thrown some dust in the mouth of the jar, carried it
away; but it was broken at the bottom, and some blood
dripping from it attracted the notice of passengers in
the street, and caused his apprehension. Some jewels
which had belonged to the murdered woman were found
upon his person.

3rd of March.—22nd of Showwál.—Saw the procession
of the Mahmal. It differed from the last which I saw,
seven years ago (in 1827), in being attended with less
pomp. First, about two hours and a half after sunrise, a
small field-piece (for firing the signals for departure after

the halts) was drawn along. This was followed by a
company of Baltageeyeh (or Pioneers), and the Báshà's
guards, with their band at their head. Then came a
train of several camels with large stuffed saddles, upon
the forepart of which were fixed two small flags, slanting
forwards, and a small plume of ostrich-feathers upon the
top of a small stick placed upright. These camels were
dyed red, with hennà; and had housings ornamented with
small shells (cowries): some were decorated with palm-
branches, fixed upright upon the saddle: some had a large
bell hung on each side; and some bore a pair of the large
kettle-drums called nakákeer, with the man who beat them.
The *takht'rawa'n* of the Emeer El-Hágg (or Chief of the
Pilgrims) followed next, borne by two camels. Then
came numerous groups of darweeshes, with the banners
of their several orders (flags, poles, nets, &c.) : some of
them repeating the name of God, and nodding their heads;
and some beating, with a leather strap, a small kettle-drum,
which they held in the left hand. Among these groups
were two swordsmen, who repeatedly engaged each other
in a mock combat; two wrestlers, naked to the waist, and
smeared with oil ; and the fantastical figure described in
my account of the procession of the Kisweh,* mounted on
a horse, and clad in sheep-skins, with a high skin cap, and
a false beard. The darweeshes were followed by the
Mahmal; which has but a poor appearance this year; the
covering being old, and its embroidery tarnished. The
people crowded to touch it with their hands, or with the

---

* Cp. *Mod. Eg.* pp. 481, ff.

end of a shawl; several persons unwinding their turbans,
and women at the windows taking off their head-veils,
for this purpose. I had been freely allowed to examine
and handle it when it was deposited in the mosque of the
Ḥasaneyn. The half-naked sheykh whom I have mentioned
in my account of the procession of the Kisweh, and in that
of the former procession of the Maḥmal, followed the sacred
banner, as usual, mounted on a camel, and rolling his head.
Some soldiers, with the Emeer el-Ḥágg and other officers
who accompany the caravan, closed the procession. In
less than an hour, the whole procession had passed the
place where I sat.

Many of the shop-keepers in the principal sooḳs (or
bázárs) are painting their shops in a rude kind of European
style, decorating the shutters, &c., with flowers and other
ornamental devices, painted on a light blue ground. The
appearance of these streets may now be compared to that
of an old Oriental garment, remarkable for the peculiarity
of its form and work, patched over with pieces of European
printed calico. I am sorry to observe that Maṣr is not
only falling to decay, but that it is rapidly losing that uni-
form and unique style of architecture which has so long
characterized it. Most of the new houses of the grandees
and even of persons of moderate wealth, are built in the
style of Constantinople; with shelving roofs and glass
windows.—One of my friends here remarked to me that
the painting the shops blue was a sign of some heavy
calamity being about to befal the city: blue (but really of
a very *dark* shade) being the colour of mourning. Another
observed that these shops resembled the person who recom-

mended their decoration (the Báshà); being fair without, but mean and dirty within.

There has been much talk here for some weeks past (ever since my arrival) of a project which the Báshà is about to put in execution, and which was at first said to be nothing less than the obstruction of the river by a dam to be thrown across it a few miles below the metropolis, in order to throw the whole tide of the river into the canals, and so to irrigate Lower Egypt more effectually: but latterly the real intention of the Báshà has become better known. The two branches of the Nile which enclose the Delta are to flow under two bridges, to be constructed a little below the point where the river divides, each in the neck of a peninsula formed by a bend of the river; across which neck or isthmus a new bed for the water is to be made as soon as the bridge is completed; after which the old bed surrounding the peninsula is to be filled up. These two bridges are to be connected with each other, and with Es-Suweys (or Suez) on the one side and Alexandria on the other, by a rail-road. The difficulty of the undertaking is immense; for these bridges are to withstand the tremendous tide of the inundation, and occasionally to be closed by flood-gates, so as to increase the height of the river above sufficiently to cause it to fill all the small canals by which the Delta and the adjacent provinces are irrigated. A similar undertaking was projected by Bonaparte, when here.

18th April.—9th Zu-l-Ḥeggeh.—This is the Day of the Pilgrimage; that is to say, of the six-hours' journey from Mekkeh to Mount 'Arafát, which gives to each person who

performs it the title of Pilgrim, and without the perform-
ance of which he would not obtain that title even if he
had journeyed to Mekkeh from the most remote part
of the Muslim world.   The halt upon Mount 'Arafát
happening this year on a Friday, the Sabbath of the
Muslims, has made several of my friends express great
regret that they have been unable to perform the pilgrimage under such a propitious circumstance.

19th.—The 'Eed el-Kebeer.—Nothing unusual to remark upon.

May 25th.—We were somewhat alarmed to-day, about
an hour after noon, by a shock of an earthquake.   I was
three times, with less than a moment's intervention, rather
violently shaken on my seat; and several long cracks were
opened in the walls of the house in which I am living.
I have heard of no house having been thrown down or
much injured by it.   It is supposed to have shown its
greatest violence (that is, to have originated) in Syria.

June 7th.— During the week which is now closing all
classes of courtesans, including the *ghawázee* (or public
dancing-girls), have been suppressed in the metropolis and
its neighbourhood.   This measure has been talked of, as
about to be put in execution, for some months past.   The
courtesans had become extremely numerous, and were
scattered in every quarter of the town ; some of them
living in houses almost fit to be the residences of
grandees ; and acquiring considerable wealth.

July 29th.—Went to the Pyramids of El-Geezeh.
Stayed in " Caviglia's Tomb."

30th.—We again experienced a shock of an earthquake,

more violent than the former, at about half-past nine P.M. Heard of no injury done.

Aug. 2nd.—Returned from the Pyramids.

5th.—The dam of the Canal of Maṣr cut. I have given an account of this in another note-book.*

12th.—Last night, Seleem Bey, a general in the Báshà's service, hired a large party of fiḳees, to perform a recital of the Ḳur-án, in his house in this city; and then went up into his ḥareem, and strangled his wife. He had written to Ibraheem Báshà, accusing this woman (who was the daughter of a Turk in high office) of incontinence; and asking his permission to punish her. He received for answer, that he might do as he pleased. He then sent Ibraheem Báshà's letter to Moḥammad 'Alee, asking the same permission of the latter; and received the same answer. The case presents a sufficient proof of Moḥammad 'Alee's ideas of justice and humanity. Had he wished to indulge his creature with permission to exercise the utmost severity of the law, he could only have said—"If you can produce four witnesses against your wife, or if you can swear that you have witnessed her crime by the oath ordained in cases of this kind, and she will not take the same oath that the accusation is false, let her be stoned to death."

Sept. 17th.—My 33rd birth-day. I have completed, as far as I can see, my notes on the manners and customs of the Muslims of Egypt. I have only to look over them; and to ask a few questions respecting the Copts.†

---

* Cp. *Mod. Eg.* pp. 493—8.

† Here follows an account of the nine days' festival which

Oct. 27th.—I generally pay a visit to the shop of the
Báshà's booksellers on the mornings of Monday and
Thursday, when auction-markets are held in the street
where the shop is situated, and in the neighbouring bázár
of Khán El-Khaleelee (the chief Turkish bázár) which
occasion the street above-mentioned to be much crowded,
and to present an amusing scene: but I am often more
amused with the persons who frequent the shop where
I take my seat.   When I went there to-day, I found there
an old man who had been possessed of large property in
land; but had been deprived of it by the Báshà, and been
compelled to become a member of the university, the
great mosque El-Azhar.   This man, the Hágg . . . . . ,
is a celebrated character.   He rendered great assistance,
both by his wealth and by active service, to Mohammad
'Alee, in his contest with his predecessor, Khursheed
Báshà, when the latter was besieged in the Citadel.   The
greater part of his property was confiscated by the man
he had thus served, through fear of his influence.   He
thus shared the fate of most of those who had rendered
eminent services to Mohammad 'Alee; but he contrived
to hide much of his wealth; and has since employed friends
to trade with it privately on his account, so that he has
still a large income; but the third part of his receipts he
always gives to the poor.   The elder of the two booksellers was relating his having just purchased a house.
There lived next-door to him, he said, a fikee, a member

took place on the marriage of the sister of Aḥmad Báshà; cp.
Mrs. Poole's *Englishwoman in Egypt,* vol. iii. pp. 61—77.

of the Azhar, and of some repute; to whom 14 ķeeráṭs
(or 24th parts) of the house in which he (the fikee)
lodged belonged: the other 10 ķeeráṭs of this house
belonged to a tailor. The bookseller's house was entered,
from the roof, and plundered, three times, of wheat, butter,
&c. The fikee was accused by the bookseller of having
committed these thefts; and confessed that he had; urging,
in palliation, that he had only taken his food. The bookseller caused him to be imprisoned in the Citadel; and,
after he had been confined there many days, offered to
procure his liberation if he would sell him the above-
mentioned share of his house. This was done; it was sold
for six and a half purses. The bookseller then wanted to
procure the tailor's share; and proposed to him to repair
or separate or sell: for the house was in a ruined state.
The tailor, refusing to do either, was summoned to the
Ķádee's court, and compelled to sell his share; for which
he demanded five purses. Having received this sum of
money, he met, on his way home, a friend, whom he told
what he had done. "You fool"—said his friend—"you
might have asked ten purses, and it would have been
given." The tailor threw down the purse in the middle
of the street; kicked off his shoes; and for several minutes
continued slapping his face, and crying out, like a woman,—
"O my sorrow!" He then snatched up the purse, and
ran home with it, crying in the same manner all the
way; and leaving his friend to follow him with his shoes.—
Soon after the bookseller had told this story, there joined
us a Persian darweesh, whom I had often met there before,

and a fat, merry-looking, red-faced man, loaded with
ragged clothing, showing the edge of a curly head of
hair below his turban, and carrying a long staff. Everybody at the shop, excepting myself, kissed his hand: he
offered me his hand, and, after taking it, I kissed my
own, and he did the same. I was informed that he was
a celebrated saint. He took snuff; smoked from my pipe;
and had a constant smile upon his countenance; though
he seldom spoke: almost the only words he uttered were
a warm commendation of an answer which I gave to the
Persian: on his (the Persian's) asking me why I had not
already departed from Masr as I had intended, I said that
the servant of God was passive and not elective; and this
sentiment, though common, seemed much to please the
welee: he repeated it with emphasis.—There next joined
us a man of a very respectable and intelligent appearance,
applying for a copy of the sheykh Rifá'ah's visit to France,
lately printed at Boolák. Asking what were the general
contents of this book, a person present answered him, that
the author relates his voyage from Alexandria to Marseilles;
how he got drunk on board the ship, and was tied to
the mast, and flogged; that he ate pork in the land of
infidelity and obstinacy, and that it is a most excellent
meat; how he was delighted with the French girls, and
how superior they are in charms to the women of Egypt;
and, having qualified himself, in every accomplishment,
for an eminent place in Hell, returned to his native country.
This was an ironical quizz on the sheykh Rifá'ah for his
strict conscientious adherence to the precepts of El-Islám

during his voyage and his residence in France. The applicant for this book had a cataract in each of his eyes. I advised him to seek relief from the French surgeon Clot Bey; but he said that he was afraid to go to the hospital; for he had heard that many patients there were killed and boiled, to make skeletons: he afterwards, however, on my assuring him that his fears were groundless, promised to go.—While I was talking with him, there began to pass by the shop a long funeral-train, consisting of numerous fikees, and many of the 'Ulamà. On my asking whose funeral it was, I was answered, "The sheykh El-Menzeláwee," sheykh of the Saạdeeyeh darweeshes. I was surprised; having seen him a few days before in apparently good health. Presently I saw him walking in the procession. I asked again; and was answered as before. "Why," said I, "praise be to God, the sheykh is walking with you, in good health:" I was then told that the deceased was his wife. Some Saạdeeyeh in the procession were performing a zikr as they passed along; repeating "Allah!" When the bier came in view, I heard the women who followed raising their *zagha'reet,* or cries of joy, instead of lamenting. The deceased was a famous saint. She was the sister of the late sheykh of the Saạdeeyeh; and it is believed that her husband, the present sheykh, derived his miraculous powers from her. It is said that she prophesied yesterday the exact hour of her death this day. The women began to lament when the corpse left the house; and, as usual when this is done at the funeral of a saint, the bearers declared that they could not move it: as soon as the lamentations

were changed to the cries of joy, the bearers pretended
to find their work quite easy.*

Nov. 6th.—To-day, as I was sitting at the booksellers'
shop, a reputed welee, whom I have often seen, came and
seated himself by me, and began, in a series of abrupt
sentences, to relate to me various matters respecting me,
past, present, and to come. His name is the sheykh
'Alee el-Leysee. He is a poor man, supported by alms :
tall and thin and very dark ; about thirty years of age ;
and wears nothing, at present, but a blue shirt and a
girdle, and a padded red cap. " O Efendee ! " he said,
"thou hast been very anxious for some days. There is
a grain of anxiety remaining in thee yet. Do not fear.
There is a letter coming to thee by sea, that will bring
thee good news. [He then told Lane that all his family
were well except one, who was then suffering from an
intermittent fever, which was proved afterwards to be
true.] . . . . I wanted to ask thee for something
to-day ; but I feared : I feared greatly. Thou must be
invested with wiláyeh" (i. e. be made a welee): " the
welees love thee ; and the Prophet loves thee. Thou must
go to the sheykh Mustafà El-Munádee, and the sheykh
El-Baháee ! " (These are two very celebrated welees).
"Thou must be a welee." He then took my right hand,
in the manner which is practised on giving the covenant
which admits a person a darweesh, and repeated the
Fát'ḥah ; after which he added, " I have admitted thee

* Cp. notes to the *Thousand and One Nights*, 2nd ed., ii.,
p. 64.

my darweesh." Having told me of several circumstances
relating to me, some of which he had doubtless learned of
persons acquainted with me, and which I could not deny,
and some which time only will prove true or false, he
ventured at a further prophecy and hazardous guessing;
and certainly his guessing was wonderful; for he informed
me of matters relating to my family which were perfectly
true, matters of an unusual nature, with singular minute-
ness and truth; making no mistake as far as I yet know.
He then added—"To night, please God, thou shalt see
the Prophet (Moḥammad) in thy sleep, and El-Khiḍr,
and the seyd El-Bedawee. This is Regeb; and I wanted
to ask of thee—but I feared—I wanted to ask of thee four
piasters, to buy meat and bread and oil and radishes.
Regeb! Regeb! I have great offices to do for thee
to-night." Less than a shilling for all that he promised
was little enough. I gave it him for the trouble he had
taken; and he muttered many abrupt prayers for me.*—
It is just a year, to-day, since I embarked in London
for this country.

7th.—I saw, in my sleep, neither Mohammad nor
El-Khiḍr nor the seyd El-Bedawee; unless, like Nebu-
chadnezzar, I cannot remember my dreams. The welee,
therefore, I fear, is a cheat.

11th.—The Turkish pilgrims are beginning to arrive,
in considerable numbers.—Four men were beheaded to-day,
for repeated robberies and murders.

---

* Cp. *Thousand and One Nights*, i., p. 212.

F

18th.—Went to the Moolid of the Seyyideh Zeyneb; which I have described in note-book no. 3.*

20th.—About a hundred boys, from about 11 to 14 years of age, were conducted by my house this evening, to be enlisted. The mothers of many of them followed, screaming, and with their heads, faces, breasts, and the fore part of their clothing, plastered with mud.

22nd.—The government has given orders, which are being put in execution, to pull down the maṣṭabahs and the saḳeefehs, or coverings, of matting, in almost all the sooḳs, or bázárs, and most of the thoroughfare streets. The former are not to be rebuilt in the more narrow and more frequented streets, and in most other parts are only to be made about two spans wide. The saḳeefehs are not to be replaced unless constructed of wood. The reason for pulling down or altering the maṣṭabahs is to afford more room for the passengers, and particularly for the Báshà's carriages, and for carts which are to be employed to remove dust and rubbish. The appearance of the city is rapidly changing, and losing its Arabian aspect.

24th.—The sheykh 'Alee told me to-day that I should not yet set out on my voyage home. In the evening news arrived of the plague having broken out in Alexandria, which prevents my going as I had intended by a ship now loading. I was packing to leave Maṣr. I fear I shall be detained here until next spring or summer.

---

* Cp. *Mod. Eg.* pp. 467—8.

28th.—Witnessed the festival of the Mearág, described in note-book no 3.*

1st December.—The shopkeepers are decorating (as they call it) their shops; and most of the larger private houses, and many others, in the thoroughfare streets, are undergoing the same operation, by order of the government, in honour (it is said) of Ibraheem Báshà, who is soon expected in Masr, from Syria. Most of the shops and houses are daubed with red and white, in broad, horizontal stripes; which, being very ill done in general, must be called in truth the reverse of decoration. Others are daubed in a more fanciful and more rude style, with lines, spots, &c., of red upon a white ground; and some, with grotesque representations of men, beasts, trees, boats, &c., such as very young children in our country would amuse themselves by drawing.

26th.—I have been in Cairo just a year. I begin now to write out the fair copy of my work on the Modern Egyptians. The plague continues at Alexandria.

4th January, 1835.—The plague has spread beyond Alexandria, and to-day a Maltese, from Alexandria, died here, in the Frank quarter, of this disease. I prepare immediately to go to Thebes, to be secure from the plague, as it is expected now to spread in Cairo. Mr. Fresnel is to accompany me.

5th.—Engaged a large boat to take us to Thebes, for four hundred piasters.

---

* Cp. *Mod. Eg.* pp. 468—70.

F 2

8th.—Embarked for Thebes, in the afternoon. Proceeded to Maṣr el-'Ateekah.

9th.—Contrary wind. Remained at Maṣr el-'Ateekah.

10th.—Fine wind. Passed Rikkah in the evening.

11th.—High N. wind. Arrived at Benee Suweyf at noon. Here some fakeers, thinking us Turkish pilgrims, came and recited the Ḳur-án, for alms, by our boat. Proceeded.

12th.—Passed El-Minyeh after sunset.

13th.—Stopped before the grottoes of Benee Ḥasan at night. Early next morning landed to walk to the Speos Artemidos, which I had not hitherto seen. Took with me one of my servants (Khaleefeh, a young man), a Copt whom we had taken as a passenger to Thebes ('Abd el-Mellák), and two boatmen; one of these two boatmen was a very fine man, the other an old, fat, inactive fellow. Put my pistols in Khaleefeh's girdle; and myself carried nothing but my sword. A little above the grottoes abovementioned is a ruined and deserted village by the river. About a mile further is another ruined village partly inhabited; and about the same distance beyond this is a third village, wholly inhabited, with palm-trees. We passed the first and second villages. A little beyond the latter we turn towards the mountains, and find a wide ravine or valley, in the right or southern side of which are several grottoes along the lower part of the rock. As we approached this ravine, several groups of people came out from the second village, with nebboots; and some with guns and pistols: two groups, about a dozen altogether, followed us: we saw that we were in danger, but it was too late to retreat. The men came to us. Some went back; others came; and soon there came another group from the third village, with a man in a clean blue gown, meláyeh, and white turban: these sat a while at the entrance of the ravine, while we were within, with the other men, who spoke civilly to us, but looked exceedingly treacherous and savage. A boy who accompanied them whispered to my servant and the younger boatman to keep close to me; for that the men with him had come to take them for soldiers. As it was now impossible to escape, I began to examine the line of grottoes, and prepared to make a drawing; merely that they might not be deceived by my dress, and take me for a Turk; as Europeans are more protected now in Egypt.—Soon after I had begun to make a sketch of this excavation, for the purpose before mentioned, the party that was at the entrance of the ravine came to us; and while my back was turned, they seized my servant and the younger boatman: the pistols were snatched from the servant and discharged and carried away and one of them broken, and the two prisoners were hurried off, while two men held me to prevent my drawing my sword, which, as they truly enough said, would have been the cause of my being immediately killed. As soon as the men who had taken my servant and boatman had proceeded a few hundred yards towards the principal village, the others left me with my two remaining attendants. As quickly as I could, I gathered together my instruments, and then pursued the party who had taken my two men. On my approaching them, three of them turned back (one of

these, the chief, with the white turban, &c.), and desired
me to return. I said I should follow them to the village,
and there liberate the prisoners. Upon this, they attacked
with their long staves; and I received from the chief a
blow on my chest, which obliged me to retreat, or I should
without doubt have been killed. A boy who was with
them followed me; brought back my pistols; kissed them
twice, and, kneeling on the ground, presented them to
me. The flints were taken out. My servant and the
boatman, as I learned afterwards, were taken before the
governor of the district that same day. A woman followed
my servant, with feigned lamentations, crying, "Why do
you say you are not my son? Is not that decorated house
the house of your father? and are not those palm-trees
your father's palm-trees? and have not you eaten the red
dates?" This was to make the governor think that he
was a young man of the village, and not stolen: for a
number of men had been required from the village for
soldiers; and the people of the village had been employing
themselves in taking passengers instead. They took five
others that same day; and one of these, who attempted to
escape, they shot, in the presence of my servant.—I returned to my boat, with the intention of applying immediately to the governor (*ma-moor*) of the district. We
were informed that he was at the village of Sákiyet
Moosà, a few miles higher up the river, on the opposite
(or western) bank. On arriving there, we found that he
was at the opposite village of Esh-sheykh Timáee. The
wind was so violent that we could not cross over with
safety until the evening. We then landed there, about an

hour after sunset. Accompanied by Mr. Fresnel, I went
to his house. He was sitting with a number of attendants,
in an open-fronted room (a mak'ad) facing a court, and,
after the day's fasting (it being Ramadán), amusing
himself by listening to the chanting of a public reciter of
poetry. We entered with an abrupt and consequential
manner, necessary to be assumed on such an occasion;
and the governor rose to us, returned us the Muslim
salutation, and gave up his own place to me; for I, having
to make the complaint, was foremost. He handed me the
snake of his sheesheh; and coffee was brought. I then
made my complaint, with an air of assumed pride, shewed
our firmáns, which nobody present could read, and demanded the restoration of my servant and boatman, and
the punishment of the men who had assaulted me; particularly of him who had struck me. The ma-moor did not
confess that the servant and boatman had been brought
to him that day at Benee Hasan, which was the case;
but promised that they should be restored, and that he
would soften the feet of the men who had assaulted me.—
On the following morning the servant was brought
and given up to me; but the persons who brought him
declared to the ma-moor that the boatman had made his
escape, and that the men who had assaulted me had fled.
So that I failed in my object of punishing them and
gained but half what I wished. I found afterwards that
the man who struck me was the sheykh of Benee Hasan: had
I known this before, I could have insisted upon his being
punished; as they could not have had the impudence to say
that the sheykh would run away from his superior officer.

14th.—Having obtained the liberation of my servant, proceeded to Mellowee. Remained there the following day. — 15th. Proceeded to Gebel El-Ḳuseyr. — 17th. Becalmed under Gebel El-Ḳuseyr. Towed a little.—18th. Passed Menfeloot after sunset.—19th. Arrived at Asyoot at 1 P.M. Proceeded in the evening.—20th. Passed Aboo Teeg at 1 P.M.—21st. Passed Akhmeem in the afternoon. —22nd. Arrived at Girga. This town is much ruined since I was last here : it has suffered much from the river. Proceeded about noon. Made but little way. Saw a crocodile. — 23rd. Calm. Thermometer 73°. Proceeded by towing. Approaching the neighbourhood of Farshoot, saw nine crocodiles together, and shortly after, nineteen more.—24th. Arrived at Hoo at sunset. —25th. To Dishneh.—26th. Saw nine crocodiles on two sand-banks opposite Dendarah. Arrived at Ḳinè at night. —27th. Passed Ḳuft at night.—28th. Saw about forty vultures (most of them rakhams, but many nisrs) on a sand-bank, in the morning, near the skeleton of a crocodile : afterwards, many pelicans and cranes. Proceeded a little way by towing, and afterwards by sail.—29th. Last day of Ramaḍán. Arrived at El-Ḳurneh about 1 P.M.

It was our intention to take up our quarters in a tomb which had been converted into a convenient dwelling by Mr. Wilkinson and Mr. Hay. We found Mr. Gosset occupying one apartment of it : I have taken possession of another apartment, separated from the former by a low wall with a door ; and Mr. Fresnel has settled in a tomb just below, which was occupied by Bonomi and other artists in the employ of Mr. Hay. Our abode is in the

Hill of the Sheykh, overlooking the whole plain of Thebes. A man named 'Owad has the charge of it; and Mr. Gosset and I pay him each 15 piasters a month for his services.

April 3rd.—The Báshà has paid a visit to this part of Egypt; went as far as Isna; and has just passed us on his way down. It is said that he came to inspect the state of the agriculture and to inquire into the conduct of the local governors; which he has not done. He has caused the villages of Erment to be destroyed; and the sheep &c. of all the inhabitants and of strangers who had sent their cattle &c. thither for pasture to be confiscated; because many of the peasants of these villages could not be made to pay their taxes.

17th.—Good Friday.—A man of this place died to-day of the plague, taken by wearing the clothes of a Nubian boatman, who was landed here five days ago, ill of this disease, and placed under the sycamore at the landing-place to die; where he did die very soon after. The man of this place who died to-day was a relation of my guard; whom, as he has had intercourse with the family of the dead man, and, I am told, attended the funeral, I am obliged to dismiss for a time. Put ourselves in strict quarantine. M. Mimaut, the French Consul-General, who is staying at Luxor, put a stop next day to all communication between this side of the river and the opposite; but is to send us meat &c. every two days.

20th.—Another man of this place, a relation of the one above-mentioned, and father of Mr. Gosset's guard and water-carrier, died of the plague to-day, taken by wearing the clothes of the Nubian boatman.

May 9th.—No more deaths by plague having occurred here, we gave up our quarantine this day; having confined ourselves three weeks. The plague is said to be very severe in Alexandria; and becoming so in the metropolis.

June 25th.—The plague is said to have almost ceased in the metropolis and Alexandria in the beginning of this month. The French Consul has received intelligence that 75,000 persons have died by it in Maṣr; and that 6000 houses are completely desolated by this disease, and closed. We sent yesterday to Ḳinè, for a boat to convey us to Maṣr,—and Mr. Gosset left yesterday.

Our messengers came back from Ḳinè without having procured a boat; finding the demands for boat-hire very high, on account of the number of pilgrims on their return from the Ḥegáz. We sent again; and procured a large dahabeeyeh to convey us to Maṣr, for 650 piasters; of which I am to pay half.

30th.—Our boat arrived last night. We embarked to-day, and commenced our voyage at about 1 P.M.—1st July. Arrived early at Ḳinè. Went to the remains of Dendarah: found the first little temple destroyed; a great portion of the portal before the great temple, and part of the great temple itself, the upper part of the middle of the east side. In and about the temple were many felláheen, hiding themselves, in the fear of being taken to work in making a new canal, or of being pressed for the army. Two or three cases of cholera had occurred at Ḳinè: I heard of three deaths by this disease here: it is said to

be also in the Hegáz. Continued our voyage in the afternoon.—3rd. Arrived at Girga in the forenoon.—4th.
Passed Akhmeem, at night.—5th. Stayed most part of
the day at Gezeeret Shenduweel.—6th. Stopped at Tahta.
—7th. To Aboo Teeg. — 8th. Arrived at Asyoot, at
10 A.M.—9th. Arrived at Menfeloot, at 9 A.M. Proceeded
at noon. Menfeloot has lately been much ruined by the
inundations, towards the river.—10th. Passed Tell el-
'Amár'neh at sunset.—11th. Passed El-Minyeh after
sunset.—12th. To Aboo Girga.—13th. Passed Benee
Suweyf, at night.—14th. Saw the Pyramids of. Dahshoor
in the evening.—15th. Arrived at Masr el-'Ateekah,
at 8 A.M.: landed, and took up my abode in my former
house.

A few deaths by cholera have happened in the metropolis and its neighbourhood. Some persons say that the
plague has not yet quite ceased here. It has destroyed a
third, or more, of the population of the city; about 80,000
persons; chiefly young persons, between 10 and 25 years
of age; and most of these females. It has also been
particularly fatal to Franks and other foreigners. 6000
houses here have been desolated by it; and are closed.
In riding through the whole length of the metropolis,
from south to north, I saw so few people in the streets
compared with the number I used formerly to see, and so
few shops open, that I should have thought that more
than half the inhabitants had been destroyed. This is
partly to be accounted for by the fact of many persons
having fled to the country to escape the plague.—Last
Friday, a number of persons spread a report that many

of the victims of the plague had been buried alive (in trance), and numerous women, children, and others, went out to one of the great burial-grounds to disinter their relations and friends, taking with them bread, water-melons, &c., for them. Several tombs were opened. Some ignorant people even believed that the general resurrection was to take place on that day. The plague is still in Alexandria; but slight; two or three cases a day.

16th.—To-day, being Thursday, when lamentations are renewed for persons not long dead, I was awoke early from my sleep by wailings in several houses around me. A few persons still die of the plague here. These cases are of persons attacked by the disease some days ago; a week or more. No new cases are heard of.

20th.—Exaggerated reports are spread respecting the cholera here. It makes but little progress: the deaths not ten a day. The plague is very severely raging at Dimyát.

———

The journal ends with two stories of the Plague noted on August 1st and 2nd. Shortly after this Lane returned to England, carrying with him the manuscript of certainly the most perfect picture of a people's life that has ever been written, his "Account of the Manners and Customs of the Modern Egyptians."

1835—1842.

"THE MODERN EGYPTIANS"—"THE THOUSAND AND ONE
NIGHTS."—"SELECTIONS FROM THE KUR-ÁN."

THE first thing that occupied Lane's attention
on his return to England was naturally to put
the final touches to his book and to see it through
the press. What with the ordinary delays of
printers, and the time needed for the preparation
of the wood-cuts, which he drew with his own
hand on the blocks, the work was not published
till December, 1836, by Mr. Charles Knight, who
had bought the first edition from the Society for
the Diffusion of Useful Knowledge.

Those who had advised the Society in the
matter had no cause for disappointment in the
success of the book. The first edition, in two
volumes, was wholly bought up by the booksellers within a fortnight of its publication. The
second, the Society's, was to be much cheaper,

and was therefore held back until the market was entirely cleared of the first. In 1837, however, it was brought out and stereotyped, with a first impression of four thousand copies, which were speedily disposed of. Two thousand five hundred copies in addition were struck off from the plates, and continued to be sold long after other and better editions had been issued. A third and revised edition, also in two volumes, was published by Mr. Knight in 1842. In 1846 the book was added to the series of "Knight's Weekly Volumes." Five thousand copies were printed, and half this large issue was sold by 1847. In 1860 my father, E. Stanley Poole, edited the work again, in a single volume, for Mr. Murray, with some important additions; and from this, which must be regarded as the standard edition, a reprint in two small volumes was produced by Mr. Murray in 1871, and is now almost exhausted. Altogether, nearly seventeen thousand copies of the "Modern Egyptians" have been sold, a sufficient evidence of its popularity in England. If it is added, that a German translation was almost immediately produced, with the author's sanction, and that editions have been published in America, some idea will be formed of the European and trans-Atlantic repute of the book.

The reviewers, who do not always echo the popular sentiment, were in this case singularly unanimous in their praise. A feeble but well-meant critique in the "Quarterly Review" could find no fault except with Lane's way of spelling Oriental names, which the reviewer travestied and then pronounced pedantic: the substance of the book met with his unqualified admiration. So it was with, I think, all the criticisms that appeared on the work. It was universally pronounced to be a masterpiece of faithful description.

Oriental scholars, it need hardly be said, received it with acclamation. The distinguished Arabist Fresnel, after a long residence in Egypt, wrote to Lane from Cairo in 1837: "I have read with a great deal of interest some of your chapters on the Modern Egyptians and felt immensely indebted to you for making me acquainted with so many things of which I should have remained eternally ignorant, had it not been for your *Thesaurus*." The following extract from my father's preface to the fifth edition explains very clearly in what the value of the work lies. If they are the words of a near kinsman, they are also those of an accomplished Arabic scholar and one who had lived long in Egypt.

" Of the Modern Egyptians, as the work of an Uncle and Master, it would be difficult for me to speak, were its merits less known and recognised than they are. At once the most remarkable description of a people ever written, and one that cannot now be re-written, it will always live in the literature of England. With a thorough knowledge of the people and of their language, singular power of description, and minute accuracy, Mr. Lane wrote his account of the 'Modern Egyptians,' when they could, for the last time, be described. Twenty-five years of steam-communication with Egypt have more altered its inhabitants than had the preceding five centuries. They then retained the habits and manners of their remote ancestors:

they now are yearly straying from old paths into the new ways of European civilization. Scholars will ever regard it as most fortunate that Mr. Lane seized his opportunity, and described so remarkable a people while yet they were unchanged.

" A residence of seven years in Egypt, principally in Cairo, while it enabled me to become familiar with the people, did not afford me any new fact that might be added to this work: and a distinguished English as well as Biblical scholar, the Author of 'Sinai and Palestine,' not long ago remarked to me, 'The Modern Egyptians is the most provoking book I ever read: whenever I thought I had discovered, in Cairo, something that must surely have been omitted, I invariably found my new fact already recorded.' I may add that a well-known German Orientalist [Dr. Sprenger] has lately visited Cairo with the express intention of correcting Mr. Lane's descriptions, and confessed that his search after mistakes was altogether vain."*

---

* E. Stanley Poole, Editor's Preface to 5th [Standard] Ed. *Modern Egyptians.*

G

After the "Modern Egyptians" had been published, and his time was once more his own, Lane
employed himself in that favourite amusement
of learned men, attending the meetings of
societies. These bodies, however, had more life
in them forty years ago than now, and their
proceedings had not yet approached that de-
batable border line between learning and futility
which has now been successfully crossed. The
Asiatic Society, which still produces some good
work, was then under the inspiriting influence of
the Earl of Munster, and the Oriental Text Committee and the Translation Fund were bringing
out that long series of works of which many are
still most valuable, although some have deservedly
died the death. At the meetings of these societies
Lane was a prominent figure. Lord Munster
regarded him as his right hand and would have
his advice on everything connected with the
work of the Committee and the Asiatic Society;
and any problem in Arabic literature, any in-
scription that defied Prof. Shakespear and the
other Orientalists of the Society, was referred
to Lane and generally decided on the spot. But

he was not a man to remain long contented
with a sort of learned kettledrum-tea existence.
He was wishing to be at work again; and the
opportunity came very quickly. In the "Modern
Egyptians" he had referred to the "The Thousand
and One Nights," or "Arabian Nights" as they
are commonly called, as forming a faithful
picture of Arab life: and the remark had drawn
more attention to the work than when it was
merely regarded as a collection of amusing and
questionably moral tales to be given to children
with due caution. Lane was asked to translate
them afresh. In his prospectus he showed that
the ordinary English version was taken from
Galland's French translation, which abounds in
perhaps every fault which the most ingenious
editor could devise for the destruction of a hated
author. It is thoroughly inaccurate in point of
scholarship; it misunderstands the simplest Arab
customs and turns them into customs of India
or Persia; it puts the whole into a European
dress which destroys the oriental glamour of the
original; and it mixes with the true Arabian
Nights others which do not belong to the collection

at all. Our English versions, based upon this,
only magnified each vice and extinguished the
few merits the work possessed in the French.

In these circumstances there could be no
question that a new translation was necessary;
and there was no man better able to translate
a work illustrative of Arab life than the author
of "The Manners and Customs of the Modern
Egyptians." Cairo in Lane's time was still
emphatically the Arab city. It had become
the sovereign centre of Arab culture when
the City of Peace was given up to the Tatar
barbarians and Baghdad was no longer the
home of the Khaleefehs. Under the Memlook
Sultáns, Cairo, and with it Arab art, attained
the acme of its splendour; and the kings who
left behind them those wonderful monuments
of their power and culture in the Mosques
of El-Káhirah left also an established order of
life, stereotyped habits of mind, and a ceremonious
etiquette, which three centuries of Turkish rule
had not yet effaced when Lane first visited
Egypt. The manners, the dwellings, and the
dress ; the traditions and superstitions, the

ideas about things in heaven above or in the earth beneath, of the actors in "The Thousand and One Nights" were those of the people of Cairo under the Memlook Sultáns: and Lane was fortunate enough to have seen them before the tide of European innovation had begun to sweep over the picturesque scene.*

Lane resolved to make his translation of "The Thousand and One Nights" an encyclopædia of Arab manners and customs. He added to each chapter a vast number of notes, which are in fact monographs on the various details of Arabian life. Never did he write better or bring together more happily the results of his wide oriental reading and of his long Eastern experience than in these Notes. The translation

---

* I do not wish this to be taken as a defence of oriental abuses. There always comes a time when picturesque rottenness must give way to enlightened ugliness. But surely it is possible to reform the Turkish misgovernment of Egypt without pulling down the mosques and the beautiful palaces of Memlook Beys which are still to be found in old corners of Cairo. Is it really a matter of necessity for a reforming Turk to wear a tightly-buttoned frock-coat? But Easterns seem to be able to copy only those peculiarities of Europeans which rightly make us a laughing-stock to the judicious savage.

itself is distinguished by its singular accuracy
and by the marvellous way in which the oriental
tone and colour is retained. The measured
and finished language Lane chose for his version
is eminently fitted to represent the rhythmical
tongue of the Arabs: and one cannot take up
the book without being mysteriously carried into
the eastern dream-land; where we converse
gravely with wezeers and learned sheykhs, or
join the drinking-bout of a godless sultán;
uncork 'Efreets and seal them up again in
their bottles with the seal of Suleymán, on
whom be peace; follow Hároon-er-Rasheed and
Jaạfar in their nightly excursions; or die for
love of a beautiful wrist that has dropped us
a kerchief from the latticed meshrebeeyeh of
the hareem. Those who would know what the
Arabs were at their best time, what were their
virtues and what their vices, may see them and
live with them in Lane's "Thousand and One
Nights."

The book came out in monthly parts in
the years 1838 to 1840. It was illustrated
profusely by W. Harvey, who succeeded in some

slight degree in catching the oriental spirit
of the tales; though his work is decidedly
the least excellent part of the book. After
the first edition, in three volumes, 1840, two
others were produced in which the publishers
sought to popularize the translation by restoring
the old ignorant spelling of the heroes' names.
All recognized the value of Lane's work, but
they still had a prejudice in favour of their old
acquaintances Sinbad and Giaffer, and could not
immediately get used to the new comers Es-
Sindibád and Jaafar. Moreover they missed
Aladdin, who even under his reformed name
'Alá-ed-deen was not to be found in Lane
at all. To obviate these objections, the publishers
produced an emasculated edition reviving all
the old mistakes and adding the inauthentic
tales. Lane, however, immediately made a strong
protest and the edition was withdrawn from
circulation. In 1859 my father brought out
the second and standard edition of the work, and
this has since been several times reprinted;
a new issue having been required this year.
Although from the size and cost of the book,

—a cost due mainly to the illustrations, which (as Lane himself thought) might well be dispensed with,—it cannot in its present form entirely drive out the miserable versions that preceded it, and that still live in the nursery: yet it is on all hands acknowledged to be the only translation that students of the East can refer to without fear of being misled. Every oriental scholar knows that the Notes are an essential part of his library.

After this translation was finished, Lane, since he could not be idle, arranged a volume of "Selections from the Kur-án," with an introduction, notes, and an interwoven commentary. The book did not appear till 1843, when its author was in Egypt and unable to correct the proofs. Consequently it is defaced by considerable typographical errors, and its publication in that state was a continual source of annoyance to Lane. The notion was an excellent one. He wished to collect together all the important doctrinal parts of the Kur-án, in order to show what the religion of Mohammad really was according to the Prophet's own words: and he

omitted all those passages which weary or disgust
the student, and render the Kur-án an impossible book for general reading. The result is
a small volume which gives the ordinary reader
a very fair notion of the contents of the Kur án
and of the circumstances of its origin. In this
latter part of the subject there is, however,
room for that addition and improvement which
thirty years of continued progress in oriental
research could not fail to make needful: and
such alteration will be made in the new edition
which is presently to be published.

The "Selections" were but a πάρεργον. Lane
was already embarked in the great work of
his life, a work to which he devoted thirty-
four years of unintermitting labour.

1842—1849.

LANE had seemingly exhausted modern Egypt. He had described the country, drawn a minute picture of the people's life, and translated their favourite romances. But there remained before him a still greater work, one indeed not bounded to any one country but concerning the whole Mohammadan world, and yet, like his other works, having its roots in Egypt. It was no longer a popular book that he was engaged upon: it appealed only to the narrow circles of the learned. But it is the work by which his name will ever be remembered, and by which England may claim the palm of Oriental scholarship, even above Germany, the home of Eastern study in Europe.

It was impossible for Lane to acquire his in-

timate knowledge of Arabic without perceiving
the lamentable deficiencies of the materials for
its study then existing in European languages.
Especially weak were the dictionaries : for
grammar could boast the magnificent works
of De Sacy and Lumsden ; whereas in the
dictionaries of Golius and Freytag, if there were
signs of learning and industry, there was also
a dearth of material and a want of scholarship
to interpret it, still more a lack of knowledge
of Eastern minds, which resulted in statements
calculated as much to mislead as to instruct
the student. So long as the young Orientalists
of Europe were reared upon the meagre food
thus afforded to them, the standard of scholarship would be low and the number of students
limited. Lane was well aware that it was not
necessary to submit to this state of things from
a want of the means of reforming it. On the
contrary he knew that in Cairo there existed
the richest materials the Arabic lexicographer
could desire; and he determined himself to work
the quarry and to produce a thesaurus of the
language, drawn from original sources, which

should once and for all supersede the imperfect
productions of Golius and Freytag and bring
the labours and learning of the Arab lexicographers within the reach of European students.

The field into which Lane was about to throw
all his energy was a peculiar one. The materials
for composing such a work as he contemplated
were singularly perfect. For the exceptional
history of the Mohammadan Arabs had produced
a nation of grammarians and lexicologists. The
rapid spread of the tide of Muslim conquest
had threatened the corruption and even the
extinction of the language of the Kur-án ; other
tongues were beginning to intermix with the
pure Arab idiom ; and it was foreseen that,
were the process suffered to continue undis-
turbed, the sacred book of the Muslims would
soon become unintelligible to the great body
of the Faithful.

" Such being the case, it became a matter of
the highest importance to the Arabs to preserve
the knowledge of that speech which haa thus
become obsolescent, and to draw a distinct line

between the classical and post-classical language. For the former language was that of the Kur-án and of the traditions of Mohammad, the sources of their religious, moral, civil, criminal, and political code, and they possessed in that language, preserved by oral tradition,—for the art of writing in Arabia had been almost exclusively confined to the Christians and Jews,—a large collection of poetry consisting of odes and shorter pieces, which they esteemed almost as much for its intrinsic merits as for its value in illustrating their law.   Hence the vast collection of lexicons and lexicological works composed by Arabs and by Muslims naturalized among the Arabs; which compositions, but for the rapid corruption of the language, would never have been undertaken. In the aggregate of these works, with all the strictness that is observed in legal proceedings, ... the utmost care and research have been employed to embody everything that could be preserved or recovered of the classical language, the result being a collection of such authority, such exactness and such copiousness as we do not find to have been approached in the case of any other language after its corruption or decay." *

The earlier lexicographers and commentators constitute the authorities from whom all later writers have gathered their facts. They speak either of their own authority or they cite a statement—a word or a signification—illustrated often by a proverb and more frequently by a couplet, for all of which they produce what may be called a pedigree, so rigidly do they seek to exclude chance of error. " Most of the contents of the best Arabic Lexicons was committed to writing, or to the memory of students, in the latter half of the second century of the Flight, or in the former half of the next century . . . . From these and similar works, either immediately or through the medium of others in which they are cited, and from oral tradition, and, as long as it could be done with confidence, by collecting information from the Arabs of the desert, were

---

* Preface to *Lexicon*, p. viii.

composed all the best lexicons and commentaries on the classical poets, &c."* The information these lexicons impart is conveyed after the strict rules of the science of lexicology. Probably no original authorities are so thoroughly original as the works written in accordance with its rules. The writer of such a dictionary frequently says,—"I have heard an Arab of such a tribe say so-and-so," in support of a word or phrase. If he quotes from contemporaries, or from what constituted *his* original authorities, he always gives the source whence he gets his information. He is scrupulous not to assign undue weight to a weak authority. An authority was weak either because he lived after the classical age, or because he belonged to a tribe who spoke a corrupt dialect; or he might, if otherwise qualified, be known to be careless or otherwise inaccurate. The chronological limit of classicality was easily fixed. The period of classical Arabic does not extend much beyond the end of the first century of the Flight, except in the case of

---

* Preface to *Lexicon*, pp. xi., xii.

isolated tribes or rarely gifted men ; but such are always quoted with caution. They were post-Mohammadan. Even poets (and poetry is the mainstay of the Arab) born during the Prophet's lifetime were of equivocal authority. The unquestioned Arab—he who spoke the pure and undefiled tongue—was either a contemporary of Mohammad's (i. e. born before but living during his time), or he altogether preceded him and belonged to the " Times of Ignorance." The purest of the recognized tribes were generally considered to be those who dwelt between the lowlands of the coast tracts and the inhabitants of the mountains, or as Aboo-Zeyd somewhat vaguely expresses it, " the higher of the lower and the lower of the higher."*

Thus the great Arabic dictionaries were gradually compiled. To enumerate them or to attempt to distinguish their several merits is beyond my present object.† It is enough to say

---

* Cp. an excellent review of Lane's *Lexicon*, Part I., in " The Times " of March 26, 1864, written by a known hand.

† A full account of them is given in the Preface to *Lexicon*, Part I.

H

that rather more than a hundred years ago a learned dweller in Cairo, the Seyyid Murtaḍà, collected in a great lexicon, which he called the Táj-el-'Aroos, all that he deemed important in the works of his predecessors. He took for his text a celebrated dictionary, the Kámoos of El-Feyroozábádee, and wrote his own vast thesaurus in the form of a commentary upon it, interweaving the results of all the great authorities (especially the Lisán-el-'Arab) and adding from his own wide learning much that is valuable. The Táj-el-'Aroos is, in fact, a combination of all the leading lexicons, and as such, and being compiled with great care and accuracy, is unquestionably the chief and best of native Arabic dictionaries.

During his former residence in Egypt Lane had become aware of the existence of copies, or portions of copies, of this Thesaurus in Cairo; and the thought had come to him that herein lay the opportunity for constructing an Arabic Lexicon of a fullness and accuracy never yet dreamt of. To compose a work in English from the Táj-el-'Aroos would be, he saw, to provide the scholars of Europe with an authority once and for ever, from which there could be no appeal. But to attempt such a work would require another residence in Cairo, tedious and expensive transcribing of the Táj, long years of toil, and the wearisome labour of proof-sheets. And when done, who could be found to venture to publish so vast a work, involving peculiar printing at ruinous cost ?

The days of patronage were over : authors no longer waited in the vestibules of great men with odes and dedications. But the spirit that prompted the finest patronage still existed. There were those among the noblemen of England who were ready to devote their wealth to the cause of culture and learning, and who were emulous of promoting a great work that could not advance without their help. In his first visit to Egypt Lane had met Lord Prudhoe, and from that time something closer than mere acquaintance had sprung up between them. Few could know Lane without seeking to be his friend : and his worth was not that of an uncut diamond ; the courtesy

and grace of his manners were conspicuous. Lord
Prudhoe found a delight in his society which
did not vanish when they returned to England.
He would constantly come to the house in
Kensington, bringing some choice tobacco—the
only luxury Lane indulged in—and there he
would sit in the study, talking over old Eastern
scenes they had witnessed together, and discus-
sing the work then going on, "The Arabian
Nights," and Lane's plans of future study and
writing. It was during these frequent meetings
in London that the idea of the Lexicon was
talked over. Lord Prudhoe entered zealously
into the project; offered to provide Lane with
the means of collecting the materials in Cairo,
and eventually took upon himself the main
expense of the production of the work. To
understand in any degree the generosity and
public spirit evinced in this, it must be remembered that it was no ordinary book, costing
a few hundred pounds, that was thus to be
produced. It involved the employment for
thirteen years of a learned scholar in Cairo,
to transcribe the manuscript of the Táj-el-'Aroos;

it required peculiar type to be designed and cast; it demanded skilled compositors of special acquirements ; and finally, it was not a work of ordinary size, but one of eight large quarto volumes with three columns in the page, reaching when completed probably to four thousand pages. To give more precise details of the expense of the work would be an impertinence to the princely generosity that took no count of the cost. From first to last the Lexicon was the care of Lord Prudhoe. In 1847 he succeeded his brother as fourth Duke of Northumberland, but the serious addition to his duties caused by this and by his acceptance of a place in the Cabinet brought about no change in his interest in Lane's work. He would come almost yearly to Worthing to see my Uncle and learn from himself how "the great book" went on. Of the many who regretted His Grace's death in 1864, few lamented it more deeply than Lane. It was the severing of a long friendship, and a friendship which the generosity of the Duke, instead of destroying, as is the manner with the meaner sort of men, had cemented. But the bright example of the Duke created its own reflection. That support which for nearly a quarter of a century, " with a kindness and delicacy not to be surpassed," he had accorded to Lane's great undertaking was at once and at her own express wish* continued by his widow, Eleanor, Dowager Duchess of Northumberland; and to Her Grace's munificence it still owes its further publication.

The financial difficulties of the work being now overcome, Lane resolved on an instant departure for Egypt. His two previous visits had been solitary : but now he went surrounded by his family,—his wife, a Greek lady whom he had married in England in 1840, and his sister, Mrs. Poole, with her two sons, to whom he ever bore himself as a father,—just as he did twenty-five years later to two nephews of the next generation. A great sorrow had lately come upon them in the death of Lane's mother.

---

* On the death of Duke Algernon, his successor, formerly Lord Beverley, immediately offered to continue the support of the work; and his son, the present Duke, has shown an equal interest in it.

In old age her intellect was as bright, her
character as firm and tender, as they had ever
been. To her sons and daughter she was as
an angel from heaven. Over her youngest son,
though he had lived among strange peoples and
passed through dangers by sea and by land,
and was now a man on whom the eyes of the
learned waited, this gentle woman still exercised
that supreme influence which had inspired him
when a boy with the noble principles and pure
aspirations of the Higher Life; and to the last
he rendered her the same love and obedience
he had given as a child. It was this sore trouble
that decided Mrs. Poole, who had lived in late
years always with her mother, on accompanying
her brother to Egypt, and from this time to
his death she never left him for more than a
few days at a time, unless summoned by the
illness of her own sons.

In June 1842 the little party of five returned
to London from Hastings, whither they had
removed in the autumn of the preceding year;
and on July 1st they sailed for Alexandria in
the Peninsula and Oriental Company's Steam-

ship "Tagus," in itself an agreeable contrast to the small sailing vessels in which Lane had hitherto travelled, but still more pleasant in consequence of the special instructions of the Directors of the Company as to the comfort of their distinguished passenger. On July 19th they reached Alexandria, whence after a day or two they sailed up the Mahmoodeeyeh for Cairo. At first the whole party, but especially the two boys, then only twelve and ten years old, were so ill that it became doubtful whether a return to England were not the only remedy. The seasoning sickness, however, passed away, and on arriving at Boolák on July 27th Lane began again to look for a house, taking up quarters meanwhile at the Consul-General's residence, which Col. Barnet (like Mr. Salt on a former occasion) had courteously placed at his service. It was not till three weeks later that a suitable house could be found, and from the one they then entered, in the Darb-el-Gemel, their servants, and therefore themselves, were driven, after a determined resistance of two months, by a series of extraordinary sounds

and sights, which the Muslim servants attributed
to the haunting of the place by a Saint and
an 'Efreet, and which have not yet received a
satisfactory explanation.* Being at length fairly
expelled, like many people before and after them,
they took refuge (in January 1843) in a house
in the Hárat es-Sakká-een, where they remained
till the beginning of 1845, when they once more
removed, to the Kawádees, where they lived till
their return to England in 1849.

It was a pleasant little society they entered
into, for the seven years of their stay in
Cairo : but it was too changing for strong
friendships. There were it is true some kindly
people always living in Cairo : such as the
English Missionary Mr. Lieder, and his good-
natured wife ; the English physician Dr. Abbott,
to whose friendly services Lane owed much,
and not least the Consul Mr. Walne. And for
a long time Fulgence Fresnel was in Cairo
and constantly with his fellow Orientalist, for

---

* For an account of the really curious phenomena exhibited
in this house see Mrs. Poole's *Englishwoman in Egypt*, i. pp.
70—78, 199—204 ; ii. pp. 1—2.

whom he felt the affection of a brother. Mr. J. W. Wild, too, now the greatest authority on Arab art, was a very welcome addition to the little circle of friends, and it was perhaps partly his long association with Lane that opened his eyes to the beauty of Arab, as distinguished from Moresque, architecture. And the latter part of their stay was brightened by the accession of two special friends,—Sir James Outram, the Bayard of India, who was never tired of coming to the house in the Kawádees; and the Hon. Charles Murray (now the Rt. Hon. Sir Charles Murray, K.C.B.), who had succeeded Col. Barnet as Consul-General, and who from the moment of his arrival exerted himself in every way to shield Lane from the importunate visits of passing travellers and to find amusement for my father and uncle, to whom he showed unvarying kindness. Among the Alexandrians, too, who constantly visited Cairo, Lane had found good friends, especially in the late Mr. A. C. Harris, Mr. Alexander Tod and his wife, and Mr. and Mrs. Batho.

But with these exceptions the society around

them was ever on the ebb and flow, as the
season for visiting Egypt went and came again.
Of the many travellers who came to see the
country, or passed through it on the way to
India, not a few had introductions to Lane,
and the acquaintance once made was not likely
to be dropped so long as they remained in
Cairo and the Friday receptions at Lane's
house continued. This day, the Sabbath of
the Muslims, was set aside for receiving the
calls of his Muslim and other friends, and
his wife and sister used to see the Europeans
who came, in the Hareem rooms; so that on
this day there was always a double reception.
On different Fridays many of the most distinguished Orientalists of Europe and learned
Easterns might be found in Lane's study—
Lepsius, Wilkinson, Dieterici, D'Abbadie, Fresnel,
Pruner, and others; with Sheykh Mohammad
Eiyád, the Sheykh Rifá'ah, Hággee Hasan
El Burralee the poet, and other literati of
Cairo, who delighted to converse with the
Englishman who had more than once decided
the moot-points of the Ulamà of the Azhar;

whilst the less exclusively Oriental friends, and the few ladies who visited Cairo, such as Harriet Martineau, would betake themselves to the other side of the house, where Mrs. Lane and Mrs. Poole were "at home."

Except on Fridays Lane denied himself to everybody, unless unusual circumstances made the interruption a necessity. On Sundays he never allowed himself, however much pressed for time, to continue his week-day work; nor did he like Sunday visitors. On all other days he devoted himself uncompromisingly to the preparation of his Lexicon. From an early breakfast to near midnight he was always at his desk, the long hours of work being broken only by a few minutes for meals—he allowed himself no more—and a scanty half-hour of exercise, spent in walking up and down a room or on the terrace on the roof. For six months together he did not cross the threshold of his house; and during all the seven years he only once left Cairo, and that was to take his wife and sister for a three days' visit to the Pyramids. At first he used to devote a short time every

day to the classical education of his nephews,
but even this was taken off his hands after
a time by the kindness of the Rev. G. S. Cautley
and the ready counsel of Mr. Charles Murray.
But Lane continued to direct their studies, and
it was by his advice that the elder devoted
himself to the subject of modern Egypt and
thus became a distinguished Arabic scholar,
whilst the younger turned his attention to
the ancient monuments, and, twice ascending
the Nile and annotating Lane's earliest work,
laid the foundations of his reputation as an
Egyptologist.

The Lexicon was indeed begun in earnest.
The first thing to be done was the transcription of the Táj-el-'Aroos, and for this
purpose Lane before leaving England had
already consulted Fresnel, who was then living
in Cairo, and who, after careful investigation,
recommended the Sheykh Ibráheem Ed-Dásookee
for the work. The copyist must be able to
do more than merely write the Arabic character,
it need scarcely be said; he must understand
the original as a scholar, and he must hold

such a position among the learned of Cairo that he can be trusted with the manuscripts from the Mosques. Such a man was the Sheykh Ed-Dásookee; ill-tempered and avaricious, but still the right man for the work. Lane at first hoped to obtain the loan of at least large portions of the manuscript from the Mosque of Moḥammad Bey. The Páshà himself, Mohammad 'Alee, was anxious to further the work by any means in his power, and the Prime Minister, Arteen Bey, called upon Lane with the view of discovering in what manner the Government could assist him. But the loan of manuscripts from the Mosques was a request beyond the power even of Mohammad 'Alee to grant; and Lane had to submit to the tedious process of borrowing through his Sheykh a few pages at a time, which were copied and then exchanged for a few more. Thus the transcription went on; and much of Lane's time was occupied in collating it with the original and in reading and annotating it in the company of the Sheykh Ed-Dásookee. But meanwhile there were other materials to be collected. It is true the main basis of the coming work was to be the Táj-el-'Aroos: but this was founded upon many other lexicons, and Lane determined so far as might be possible to verify its quotations and to take nothing at second-hand which could be obtained from the original source. Hence it was a matter of great consequence to gather together any manuscripts that could be bought in Cairo. Fresnel gave him three most valuable manuscripts, Mr. Lieder another; and by a careful watch on the book-market, by means of his old ally Sheykh Ahmad, he was fortunate enough to accumulate more than a dozen of the most renowned lexicons; and thus he was able to test the accuracy of the Táj-el-'Aroos, and to add greatly to the perfection and authoritativeness of his own work.

After a preliminary study of Arabic lexicology,— a science complicated by technical terms of varying meaning,—and so soon as a portion of the Táj-el-'Aroos was transcribed, Lane began to compose his own Lexicon from the Táj and from the other dictionaries he had

collected. Thus from year to year the work
went slowly on; collating, collecting, composing
filled each day, each month, each year. At
length the materials were gathered, the Táj was
transcribed up to a sufficiently advanced point,
and Lane felt he need stay no longer in Egypt.
So leaving Mr. Lieder to keep the Sheykh to
his work of copying,—which, now it is finished,
fills 24 large volumes,—Lane and his family
bade farewell to the friends who had risen
around them, and reaching Alexandria on the
5th October, 1849, sailed on the 16th for England,
where they arrived on the 29th.

Such is the brief account of Lane's third
visit to Egypt, and the beginning of the
Lexicon. It was a time of unremitting ex-
hausting labour : but it was a happy time.
Lane had his wife and sister with him, and
his home was brightened by two young faces,
full of the excitement and delight of their
new and marvellous surroundings. A cloud
had fallen upon them, indeed, in 1844, when
they heard of the death of the eldest brother,
Theophilus Lane ; and some days of deep

anxiety had befallen Lane when both wife and sister lay dangerously ill with cholera and typhus fever. But on the whole the seven years had been years of happiness. His sister had gained for herself a place in literature by her "Englishwoman in Egypt," his two nephews had each marked out for himself a career as an Orientalist; he himself had accomplished his purpose and gathered together the materials and begun the composition of the great work of his life.

1849—1876.

LANE returned to Europe in 1849 the acknowledged chief of Arabic scholars. As the author
of "The Modern Egyptians" his fame as the
authority upon Egypt had been established;
and his translation of the Arabian Nights had
gained him the well-earned repute of accurate scholarship. But when it became known
on what work he was now engaged and when
specimens had shown how thoroughly that work
would be done, all who had a care for learning were eager to offer their homage. As
early as 1839 the Egyptian Society had enrolled
him among their honorary members. In 1846
the German Oriental Society elected him a cor-
responding member, and in 1871 raised him
to their highest rank, that of Ehrenmitglied;

and the example of Germany was followed, at a distance, by England, in the elections to the honorary membership of the Royal Society of Literature (1858) and of the Royal Asiatic Society (1866). In 1864 a vacancy occurred in the Académie des Inscriptions et Belles-Lettres of the Institut de France, by the promotion of De Witte, and Lane was unanimously elected a Correspondent in his place ; and in 1875, on the occasion of its Tercentenary Festival, the University of Leyden accorded to him the degree of Honorary Doctor of Literature (Philosophiae Theoreticae Magister, Litterarum Humaniorum Doctor)—the only University degree he ever accepted, though not the only one offered to him. Those singular decorations, chiefly of military origin, which learned men are sometimes pleased to receive from their Sovereign, were by Lane decidedly though respectfully declined.

It was not, however, only in the matter of diplomas that a strong interest was shown in the great work my Uncle was preparing. So soon as the immense cost of the production was known, and before Lord Prudhoe had taken upon himself the expense of printing it, efforts were made, though not by the author, to obtain for it the support it needed. The Chevalier Bunsen exerted himself in a most friendly manner to gain the help of the English Universities; but, it need hardly be said, in vain. On the other hand, Germany was anxious to obtain the distinction of supporting it. At the instance of Bunsen, Lepsius, and Abeken, seconded by many others, it was agreed to offer to publish the Lexicon at the joint expense of the Prussian Government and the Berlin Academy of Sciences; and in 1846 Prof. Dieterici was sent by the King of Prussia to Cairo to consult Lane's wishes. There were, however, conditions named to which Lane " could not willingly accede; " and moreover the arrangements for publishing in England were, by the zealous exertions of his brother Richard, nearly completed. In 1848 Lord John Russell, then Premier, made the first of a series of annual grants from the Fund for Special Service, which Lord Aberdeen continued in 1853; and in 1863 the grant was changed into an annual Pension on the Civil List.

On his return to England Lane soon settled down into his old routine of work. The composition went slowly on, and the manuscript of the Táj-el-'Aroos was gradually completed and sent over. At last, when he had been twenty years at the work, Lane felt he might begin printing.* In 1863 the First Part appeared, and in two years' time the Second followed. The Third was published in 1867, and the Fourth was printed in 1870, but the whole edition of one thousand copies was unfortunately burnt before it reached the publisher, with the exception of a single copy, and the entire Part had to be printed again, and therefore did not appear till 1872. After the

---

* The admirable press of W. M. Watts (now Messrs. Gilbert and Rivington) was selected for the work, and an entirely new fount of type was cut for it from designs by my father. Only those who have corrected the proof-sheets of a large work in foreign characters know the value of accurate printing: and that my Uncle's labour was rendered as little burdensome as possible was due to the skilful care of Mr. E. Cornish, the Oriental Manager of the Firm.

necessary two years' interval Part V. was published in 1874. The Sixth Part was half-printed (as far as p. 2386) when its author died; and it has taken me a year to finish it (1877). Two Parts remain to be published, besides the Second Book, which may be estimated at one or perhaps two Parts more.

The publication of the Lexicon more than confirmed the high expectations that had been formed of it. As Jules Mohl well said, each article is a perfect monograph, recording all that can be recorded on the subject. Each statement is followed by initials indicating the authorities from which it was derived, except where Lane has interwoven, within brackets, his own remarks and criticisms. Thus the work is, in point of authoritativeness, as sufficient for the student as if he possessed all the original manuscripts from which it is compiled. And whereas in the native writers method is unknown and meaning follows meaning in no settled sequence, Lane has succeeded in arranging each article in logical order, distinguishing between primary and secondary meanings, and making the various significations of each root a connected whole, instead of a chaotic congeries of inexplicable contradictions. The value of the manner as well as of the matter was instantly recognized by the Orientalists of Europe. There was no question of rivalry: all and each were agreed absolutely to submit to an authority which they saw to be above dispute. The greatest Arabist of Germany used to send Lane from time to time monographs of his own, inscribed with the words "Unserem Grossmeister" and the like; and his homage is but an example of the reverence felt by all for the "Schatzmeister der arabischen Sprache."

But this universal appreciation of his work did not induce Lane to slacken for a moment the severe tension of his monotonous toil. He never rested on his laurels for a single day. He felt that it was a work demanding more than one lifetime, and he determined to leave as little undone as he could. After a year at Hastings he moved to the milder climate of Worthing, and during the twenty-five years he lived there he left the place but once, going to Brighton to see his old friend Outram; and nothing but severe illness could compel him to take a day's rest.

These years at Worthing were a time of constant unvarying labour,—

> " Of toil unsever'd from tranquillity,
> Of labour that in lasting fruit outgrows
> Far noisier schemes, accomplished in repose,
> Too great for haste, too high for rivalry."

My Uncle would go to his desk after an early breakfast and work for three or four hours in the morning. An early dinner then made a necessary interruption, but afterwards he would begin again without a moment's delay, and continue writing till about four o'clock, when if the weather were fine and he in fair health he would walk with some of his family for an hour or so. Then he would come back to tea, and from six to ten would again bury himself in manuscripts, when a simple supper would end the day. At first his afternoon walk extended to three or four miles; but as his strength

waned he gradually shortened the distance,
till in his last year he could only saunter
gently up and down some shady road for half-
an-hour, and even then found himself exhausted.
So too he was at last induced by the en-
treaties of his family to close his desk at
nine o'clock instead of ten; but even then
he accomplished eight hours of study in the
day. Nothing was allowed to interfere with
these hours of work. Visitors who asked for
him were strictly denied, and it was only
by calling on his wife or sister that it was
possible to see him, and then only if he was
at a point in his composition where interruption would not entail a serious delay.
Yet these rare moments were sufficient to win
for him the lasting affection of a small circle
of friends, who were never weary of offering
him every attention in their power, and far
from taking amiss his rigid seclusion endea-
voured in all ways to shield him from the
intrusion of strangers. He never called anywhere; but sometimes he would take his
afternoon stroll in the gardens of Warwick

House, where the bright society of his kindly hostesses was a delightful relief after his arduous hours of study.

One day in the week Lane closed his books. His early training had led him to regard Sunday as a day to be set apart for the things of religion, and his long sojourn in the East had in no wise weakened this feeling. In Egypt he had frequently attended the prayers at the Mosques and there comported himself in all outward appearance as a Muslim: but this was only because without thus conforming to the ways of the people he could never have acquired that knowledge of their character which he afterwards turned to so great an account. To the last he preserved the simple earnest faith of his childhood. His acquaintance with the original languages of the Old and New Testament, and his insight into Semitic modes of thought, had certainly modified his views on some of the minor points, but in the essential doctrines of Evangelical Christianity his belief never changed. But his religion was not a mere matter of intel-

lectual adhesion to a given series of dogmas:
he carried it into his every-day life. The forms
of grace at meals, to most people purely ceremonious, were to him realities, and he never
began his day's work without uttering the
Arab dedication *Bismi-lláh*—"In the name of
God." No one who came within the reach
of his influence, however great the disagree-
ment in opinion, could fail to be impressed
with the earnestness of Lane's convictions;
and few talked with him without going away
better men than they came. His high and
pure soul shone in his countenance, in his
manner, in his every word. In his presence
a profane or impure speech was an impossi-
bility: yet no one was ever more gentle with
that frailty for which the world has no pity
He was a Christian Gentleman, of a fashion of
life that is passing away.

Sunday was to Lane a day of religion rather
than a day of rest. In the morning or afternoon he would, if he were well enough, attend
the office of the Church of England. The
remainder of the day he spent chiefly in Bib-

lical study, of which as a Hebrew scholar he possessed a critical knowledge that most of our divines might have envied. But it was not as a philological amusement that he pursued his researches. To him the Bible was the guide of his life; and he used his every endeavour to understand each doubtful passage, to emend each ignorant rendering, to interpret by the light of Semitic thought those dark sayings which the Aryan translators comprehended not, and not least to discover the harmony of Scripture and science. Thus his Sundays were not a time of thorough rest, such as the severe character of his week-day work required them to be. His Biblical reading often tried him more than a day's work at the Lexicon, and the parallel lines of ordinary print weakened eyes accustomed to the flexuous writing of Arabic manuscripts.

So the years wore on. Day followed day, and year year, without seeing any change in the monotony of Lane's life. Manuscript was written, proofs came and went, volumes were published, with unvarying regularity. The Lexicon was his one occupation. The review and the essay, the offspring of the idle hours of learned men, had no attraction to a man who could not boast an idle moment. The only contributions he ever sent to a journal were two essays that appeared in the "Zeitschrift der deutschen morgenländischen Gesellschaft." * With these exceptions Lane never allowed any literary pursuit to divert him from his work. Even the revision of new editions of his earlier works demanded more time than he would spare, and he therefore left it to his nephews.

In 1867 Lane experienced one of the great sorrows of his life. He had seen both his sister's sons well advanced in their several careers: but he was destined to lose the one

---

* The first of these is entitled "Ueber die Lexicographie der arabischen Sprache," and appeared in Bd. III. SS. 90—108 (1849). It is in the form of a letter to Prof. Lepsius, and treats of the principal Arabic Lexicons, and gives specimens of Lane's own work. The other article is "Ueber die Aussprache der arabischen Vocale und die Betonung der arabischen Wörter," an excellent treatise on the pronunciation of the Arabic Vowels and on the Accent (Bd. IV. SS. 171—186, 1850).

whom he had regarded as his own successor,
the continuer of his life-work and the heir
to his fame. My father's early death struck
a heavy blow at Lane's love and hope. It
was as the loss of an eldest son. Twenty-
seven years before, he had taken to his
home his sister and her sons ; and now,
with the same unselfish readiness, he opened
his door to the three children whom my
father's death had left orphans. From this
time my Uncle's house was home and he
was a second father to me. It was no slight
sacrifice to admit three children to his quiet
life : but he never let us know that it was
a sacrifice at all. I can never forget the
patience with which he suffered all our child-
ish waywardness, the zealous sympathy with
which he entered into our plans and pleasures,
his fatherly counsel and help in our boy-
troubles, his loving anxiety in sickness. The
few moments that he could spare from his
work, which he might well have devoted to
his own recreation, were given to us. He
delighted to lead us to the studies he had

loved himself, and would bring from the stores of his memory that scientific knowledge which had formed the favourite pursuit of his boyhood. And when I had chosen for myself the same field of study to which he had devoted his life, he gave me daily that help and advice which no one could give so well; read and revised everything I wrote; and at length, when his health was failing, gave me a last proof of his trust by confiding to me the completion of his own work.

The life of the great Orientalist was drawing to its close. Frequent attacks of low fever, added to the exhaustion of chronic bronchitis, had seriously weakened a frame already enfeebled by excessive study. I seldom left my Uncle for a few weeks without the dread that I should never see him again. It was a marvel how the delicate man battled against illness after illness, never yielding to the desire of the weary body for rest, but unflinchingly persevering with the great task he had set before him. His own knowledge of his constitution, acquired by long residence in places where medical help was not to be had, served him in good stead; and his life was ever shielded by the devoted care of his wife and sister, and the friendly attention of Dr. Henry Collet, who for many years afforded my Uncle the great advantage of his constant advice; a service of love which was continued after Dr. Collet's death, with the zeal of long affection, by his son, Mr. A. H. Collet.

But the time came when there was no longer strength to withstand the approach of death. At the beginning of August, 1876, my Uncle was suffering from a cold, which presently showed signs of a serious nature. He went on with his work till Saturday the 5th; and then a decided change came over him. The weakness increased to such a degree on Sunday that he allowed me to support him about the house, though never before would he accept even the help of an arm. That evening we induced him to go early to his bed: and he never again rose from it. Two days passed in anxious watching. Every-

K

thing that love could prompt, or the affection and skill of the doctor could suggest, was done. On Wednesday evening he seemed better: it was but the last effort. Early on Thursday morning the brave loyal spirit fought its last battle, and the mind that had endured the strain of fifty years of ceaseless toil, and yet had never known decay, at last found rest.

So ended the Scholar's life. It was begun, continued, and ended, without hope of reward. For fame he cared little; money, beyond what sufficed for his modest wants, he desired not. Pure love of knowledge was the motive of his work, and to learning, unsoiled with baser aims, he dedicated a long and studious life, rich in fruits. To the world Lane must be the ideal scholar. With us who knew him his memory will live in the sweeter thought of the noble and pure heart that wrapped us in its love.

A LIST OF THE WORKS

OF

EDWARD WILLIAM LANE.

A LIST OF THE WORKS

OF

EDWARD WILLIAM LANE.

———◆———

1.—An Account of the Manners and Customs of the Modern Egyptians.

1st edition. 2 vols. royal 18mo. (Knight) .	.	1836
2nd edition. 2 vols. royal 18mo. (S.D.U.K.)	.	1837
3rd edition. 2 vols. demy 8vo. (Knight) .	.	1842
4th edition. 3 vols. (Knight's Weekly Vols.)	.	1846
5th (standard) edition (ed. by E. STANLEY POOLE).		
1 vol., medium 8vo. (Murray) .	.	1860
,, (reprinted) 2 vols. double cr. 16mo. (Murray)		1871

2.—The Thousand and One Nights.

(In monthly parts. 1838—40).

1st edition. 3 vols. royal 8vo.	.	.	.	1840
2nd edition (ed. by E. STANLEY POOLE). 3 vols.,				
medium 8vo.	.	.	.	1859

3.—Selections from the Kurán.

1st edition. 1 vol. medium 8vo.	.	.	1843
2nd edition. *(In preparation)*.			

4.—Ueber die Lexicographie der arabischen Sprache.

  (Zeitschr. d. D. M. G. iii. 90—108) . . . 1849

5.—Ueber die Aussprache der arabischen Vocale und die Betonung der arabischen Wörter.

  (Zeitschr. d. D. M. G. iv. 171—186) . . . 1850

6.—An Arabic-English Lexicon.

  Part I. 1863
  Part II.   1865
  Part III.   1867
  Part IV.   1872
  Part V.   1874
  Part VI. (Ed. by S. Lane Poole). . . 1877
  Parts VII. and VIII. and Supplement (Book II.).
          In preparation.